CLAIMING FACE

Self-Empowerment through Self-Portraiture

An Educator's Guide to Building the Powerful Link Between Creativity and A Sense of Self

by Maya Christina Gonzalez

Reflection Press

Copyright © 2010 by Maya Christina Gonzalez. All rights reserved.

Published by Reflection Press, San Francisco, California.

For more resources, information, or to subscribe to our mailing list, visit us on our website at www.reflectionpress.com.

ISBN 978-0-9843799-0-3

Library of Congress Control Number (LCCN): 2010900458

The Reflection Press logo, CLAIMING FACE™, *THE 3 RULES*, and *THE 3 RULES* symbol are trademarks of Reflection Press.

Editing, Layout, and Graphic Design by Matthew Smith

Artwork images on page 8 © Maya Christina Gonzalez

Photograph of Maya on page 9 by Lisi deHaas

To purchase many of Maya's children's books visit: www.childrensbookpress.org

Special thanks to those who contributed to our first book:

Karen Marisa for material, intellectual and emotional support and expertise in relation to our photographic needs, (KarenMarisaPhotography@gmail.com)

Dr. Miguel Lopez for his time, insight and his general compadre-ness,

And to each child who has played with me, taught me and brought me so much beautiful reflection of resilience, strength and courage through the years.

*And I have to mention that while this is my work, I could never have gotten it out into the world without the intense brilliance and hard, hard work devoted by my extremely talented partner and husband, Matthew! I've finally met my match. I love you, baby!

For Zai.

May you know your deepest self and be the strongest, best beast ever!

This life is yours, thank you for sharing it with us.

Me and Matthew love you without end.

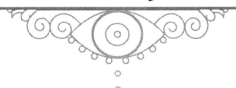

Draw it! Claim it!

Draw it! Claim it!

Draw it! Claim it!

"We are born creative beings"

"The more we free our expression the more we can know who we are"

CONTENTS

"Everyone is an Artist."

5 Expression, Standards, and Artistic Development 63

6 The 3 Rules 73

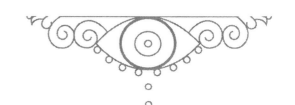

PART 2 : OUTSIDE ⟨81⟩

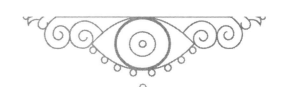

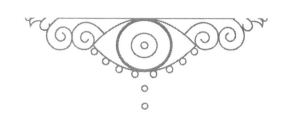

RESOURCES

"Art is always an act of courage."

"The truth is Creativity belongs to all of us."

Foreword

"You made me believe in art." - Jazmin, Age 9

The goal of the CLAIMING FACE curriculum is to build the powerful link between creativity and a sense of self. Art is the tool.

Why is this important? We are born creative beings. This is evident by the immense creative power we see in children. Every day children must find their way through new experiences, new feelings and come to their own sense of knowing. But it is conjectured that our natural creativity is progressively hindered by the perspectives and systems in our current culture. By being physically and monetarily focused, we have lost sight of one of our fundamental birthrights.

We are born creative beings for a reason. It makes us flexible, resilient, adaptable and more. My definition of creativity is: *the personal teacher within each of us. As our birthright it is the inherent ability and energy, we as humans are born with, to transcend current ideas, forms and patterns and to create meaningful new ones that are relevant to the moment and our deepest selves.*

Using art as a means of engaging with the creative process, CLAIMING FACE curriculum hopes to reclaim, retain and sustain such an important aspect of our humanity. While I see the far reaching benefits of this, my first concern is attending to those most in need in the here and now. Our children, and primarily our children who are the most marginalized.

After a lifetime of practice, I trust the power and wisdom of creativity. And in trusting creativity, I trust her greatest harbinger, children. CLAIMING FACE curriculum is designed to support all of us but especially children, to engage with creativity in order to know ourselves and be empowered to live our best lives. It is not about art, although art is made. It is about process. It is about self.

I do not believe Jazmin, the girl who wrote *"You made me believe in art,"* is talking about art in the traditional sense. Since all of my curriculum is based on self-portraiture as a tool to know and empower self, I believe it can be faithfully translated to mean *"You made me believe in myself."*

In empowering those who hold the least amount of power and influence in our society, I believe we can create a gently expanding trend of balance that may one day tip us back to deeply cherish one of our most basic tools. **Creativity.**

CREATIVITY (n.)

Creativity is the personal teacher within each of us. As our birthright it is the inherent ability and energy, we as humans are born with, to transcend current ideas, forms and patterns and to create meaningful new ones that are relevant to the moment and our deepest selves. This allows us to connect with, maintain and perpetuate flow and integrity with who we are at core.

"No one can show us ourselves more than ourselves."

"We have a need to be seen."

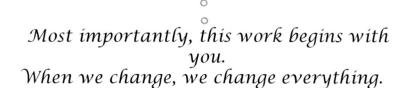

Most importantly, this work begins with you.
When we change, we change everything.

Know that as you begin this process
to know yourself more deeply,
engage with your own creative power
and claim your own face,
you will change.
You will become stronger,
more empowered,
more yourself.

Here are THE 3 RULES that will support you on your journey:

1. Everyone is an artist.
2. There is never a right or wrong way to make art.
3. Art is always an act of courage.

There is much to learn, experience, imagine, question, play, know...
whether you share this work as an educator or not,
begin here.
Everything begins with you.
I invite you to claim yourself.

I, _____ claim my face.

Draw it! Claim it!

Draw it! Claim it!

Draw it! Claim it!

"Energy is all around us and moving through us."

PART 1

INSIDE

Like life itself,
we begin INSIDE.

The origin.
The development.
How to hold the
curriculum within us.

Enter an experiential
relationship with the
curriculum.

Go inside and allow
the philosophies and
knowings to land within
you and be shaped by
your own experience
and path.

Not everything can be
verbalized or charted
out.

Some ideas must be
felt in order to be
understood.

Begin here. Enter from the inside with your own heart.

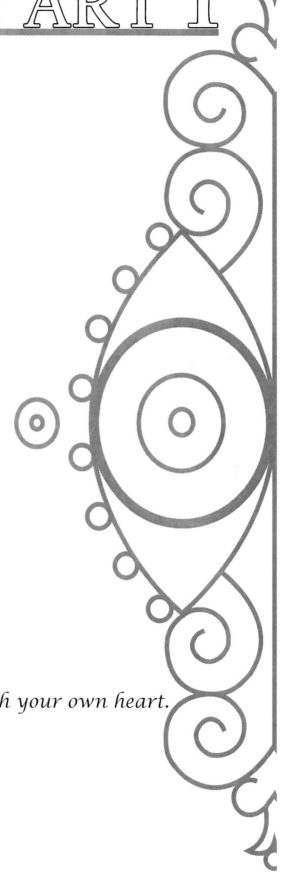

Draw it! Claim it! Draw it! Claim it!

Draw it! Claim it!

Draw it! Claim it!

CHAPTER 1

Origin & Intent of Claiming Face

I can consciously trace the origin of the CLAIMING FACE curriculum back to my childhood. Like most children I loved playing and creating everything. However, at some point making art specifically took on a deeper purpose for me. I don't know if it was born out of a deep need or was simply inherent in the wisdom and fluidity of childhood, but I began using art as a tool to affirm my existence. This set a pattern that has followed me through life.

As young as 4, I remember drawing my round, Chicana, girl face onto the blank pages in the backs of books. On some level I knew I belonged there, despite the fact that I did not see myself in any of the books I came into contact with. When I was still very young, I didn't know who I was or my place in the world, but I knew there was something about my face. I knew it was me because it was mine and no other's. As I got older and moved farther out into the world, my face became a problem to me. It felt so big, so very round, so impossible to hide. I became convinced that I had the biggest face of anyone I knew and there was nothing I could do about it. It stood out and constantly broadcast something I didn't understand; something about who I was that I could not fathom nor silence. When I moved from California to Oregon at 13, it got worse. Amidst nearly exclusively white faces, none of which were round like mine, I felt as though my face stood out even more.

Without fully realizing it, I lived with a gnawing sense of conflict and confusion about my face and what it meant, what it conveyed. Eventually I grew up to understand the world more and some of my experience came into clearer focus, which included deciphering the names I was called as a child, like *wetback, spic, beaner, chico.* I understood some of why I felt like I didn't belong, why I stood out.

As a young woman, I felt that the only way I could feel empowered would be if I totally claimed my face. Throughout my life, it was the most obvious and the most vulnerable representation of me. My big, round, Chicana, woman face. It seemed that if I claimed my own face, I was taking a step toward claiming all of myself in every deep and superficial way. In this way, my face could not be held against me, by me nor anyone else. In my early 20's I began making art in earnest. Everything was self-portraiture in some form or another as I attempted to claim my own face.

At 30, with the decision to paint full time, I moved back to California. But this time I moved to San Francisco to the predominantly Latino neighborhood of the Mission District. There, after a lifetime of invisibility, I suddenly felt recognized. I didn't stand out! In fact, I seemed to belong without effort, all because of my face. My face was not too big and round, in fact my face was perfectly normal. My face was Chicana! For the first time in my life, I could just be.

Maya, age 4

Around this time, I saw graffiti in my neighborhood that haunts me to this day. It read:

"A PEOPLE SHOULD NOT LONG FOR THEIR OWN IMAGE."

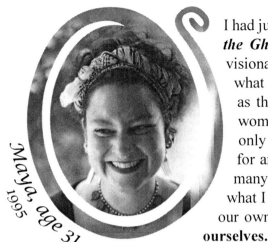

Maya, age 31, 1995

PRIETITA

I had just illustrated my first children's book, ***Prietita and the Ghost Woman*** by Gloria Anzuldua for the seminal, visionary press: Children's Book Press. After years of what I could now define as "longing," I finally felt as though I had a face and it was mine as a Chicana woman. But as amazing as this was, I noticed that not only me, but also the children I was now illustrating for and working with in the schools, still did not have many opportunities to see ourselves in our world. In fact, what I had learned was that if we didn't want to long for our own image, **we were going to have to create it for ourselves.**

As a child I used art to affirm my existence. As a young adult I used art again to affirm and claim myself. The lesson of claiming me through my face proved a long one. Through working with my own image I realized the real power of creating a reflection of myself. It allowed me to literally come face-to-face with myself. I came to reflect upon my own reflection. I got to know myself. This deeper reflection brought me a fuller experience of myself and my world. I have learned that I can look back and trust the child that I was. Without knowing, without experience, I turned to and could count on creativity. It was my greatest resource and my most immediate tool. Creativity has served me my whole life. It is a part of me as it is a part of all of us. Now I find my next step is to share what I have learned with others like myself.

Obviously, this work is very personal. I don't ever pretend that it is not. You can see that in what I share and how I teach. I don't distance. I don't want to forget that I am the children I speak to, or the adults I speak to for that matter. This keeps me honest. Because I know that in turning around to share, I continue to gather myself and create the world I dream of. I have worked very hard every step of the way. Claiming my own face has not ended. I still work at it. As I've grown and learned, my work has deepened and the basics for sharing have settled into place, including the name:
CLAIMING FACE.

I see the creative process as a container to hold us while we engage in knowing ourselves and becoming more and more empowered. For the sake of this book, I have slowed down and paid attention in order to articulate what I do when I work with children. I love working with children, but more than anything I realize I want to resource them. The best way is clearly to support you, the educator.

TO CLAIM FACE (v.)

(1) to recognize and assert one's place/face and inherent belonging in the world; (2) to embrace and celebrate what one's face expresses, how it reflects one's life and historical context in relation to ethnicity, gender expression, individuality, selfhood and more; (3) to declare and require in community the birthright to be exactly who one is inside and out; (4) to know one's self inside and out.

Inside, Outside, Process

This book is divided into **3 Parts:** INSIDE is explored in *Part One* of the book, OUTSIDE is laid out in *Part Two* and PROCESS is *Part Three*.

INSIDE. This is where we begin. In *Part One* I share personal experience and what I have learned about the power of creativity, the importance of reflection, and other practices that contribute and lend support to a strong sense of self. *Part One* explores and articulates the philosophy behind CLAIMING FACE. At the end of every chapter, you have the opportunity to *Imagine & Reflect* through creative visualizations and a series of questions. The core of *Part One* includes an exploration of the dynamic effects of presence and specifically how to use it in the classroom. *Part One* ends with a chapter about *THE 3 RULES*, which represent a distillation of the most important points of the CLAIMING FACE philosophy.

The 3 Rules

Rule #1: Everyone is an artist.

Rule #2: There is never a right or wrong way to make art.

Rule #3: Art is always an act of courage.

OUTSIDE. *Part Two* deals with the physical support of the projects. This part explores the materials and how to use them. It also explores the imagery behind my children's books and how the books can be used with the projects to connect with literacy.

PROCESS. *Part Three* is all about process. Through the support provided in *Parts One* and *Two*, *Part Three* puts the creative process into action through 26 art projects, all based on a vast and diverse sense of self-portraiture. Here you use creativity as a tool to assist yourself and your students to create reflection and better know self.

It is said that, *"All Art is Self-Portraiture."* I drive that point home through the 26 projects. It is very powerful when we create images of ourselves. But the power of the experience is multiplied when we work with actual images of ourselves through photographs. It is quite literally our face. In the projects our face (as a photograph) exists for the sole purpose of expressing something about ourselves through making art on it. We are claiming, owning, honoring, respecting our face, ourselves! This directly connects the creative process with self by using the most obvious, unavoidable, expressive part of our selves, the face, as our canvas.

Resources are compiled at the end of the book to offer further support. These include statistics about what many children are currently dealing with, additional resources arranged by topic, the CLAIMING FACE *Cheat (Please!) Sheet* and *Glossary*, and handouts to copy and use in the classroom for the projects. In the *Afterword* I share some of my personal thoughts and experiences living the curriculum.

Great care has been taken at every step to not only resource educators with different materials and experiences, but also to try and translate my experiences and how I've worked with art and creativity in the classroom. My hope is to directly support educators and students through the process that has supported me as a child and as an adult.

Who is the curriculum for?

The CLAIMING FACE curriculum is appropriate for all educators. You do not have to consider yourself an artist or even feel remotely creative. In fact, the less creative you feel, the more appropriate this is for you. It is for anyone who feels like using it. We can all benefit from investing in a stronger sense of self and engaging with the creative process. The only thing you need is **curiosity**. My experience is that the CLAIMING FACE projects can be adapted to any age. I have used them with children from 3 years old to 18 years old, and from student-teachers to university professors.

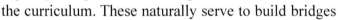

"I believe all people want to be an artist"

(From a note sent to me by a 3rd grade student with whom I got to work with every month for a year)

The curriculum inherently embodies many elements to inspire an educator to work with it. If you are a white educator working predominantly with students of color, CLAIMING FACE can serve to increase you and your classroom's cultural capacity. Respect and a strong sense of self are root elements to the curriculum. These naturally serve to build bridges between cultural differences in learning, knowing and relating. When you feel stable and respected in yourself and your life you have a foundation from which to expand and network.

CLAIMING FACE is a powerful tool for educators searching for reflection with their students. When you do the curriculum alongside your students, the powerful possibility of *Universal Reflection* exists. When direct visual or cultural reflection is not possible between educator and student, you can establish reflection through action: both educator and student do the projects. Through this kind of

UNIVERSAL REFLECTION (n.)

Reflection is usually defined as an image or representation. Reflection becomes Universal when it is not dependent on image, but on action between two or more people. For example, when the educator and the student both do the Claiming Face projects, they create a Universal Reflection of each other both being engaged in the creative process.

reflection, the projects themselves serve as a unifying and supportive experience as you inspire and encourage each other.

Since imagery is used as the tool to empower, language can be secondary if necessary. This opens up other ways of sharing and communicating which supports working with students with a language difference. Language and literacy can evolve in a more personally relevant way by connecting the imagery the student creates with the imagery in my children's books.

At all times, CLAIMING FACE helps to dismantle and renegotiate the various power imbalances present in our current culture, for example in relation to class, race, gender and more. By establishing and perpetuating a model of equality, new ways of thinking and being in relation to self, as well as others, can be explored.

In general, CLAIMING FACE is a positive choice for educators specifically looking to build a strong sense of self in themselves and/or in their students. Through self-portraiture everyone acknowledges, honors and retains their individuality. For students especially, this paves the path to learning any subject with greater confidence. A teacher in Oakland, California says, *"the children I teach are more likely to be productive members of society if they have a strong sense of self to accompany their mastery of the (academic) curriculum."*

"The curriculum is intended to empower and support educators whether you take it into the classroom or not."

The CLAIMING FACE curriculum is intended to empower and support educators whether you take it into the classroom or not. Overall, educators who enhance their ability to reflect increase their ability to understand everything from themselves and their students, to the state of education. Understanding and contextualizing self and students within the current culture helps teachers creatively re-envision their role in the classroom, in schools, and in our local and global communities. Educators are in a distinctly powerful and influential position. To empower educators is to take an important step toward putting the power of education in the hands of those who literally hold it every day.

How to use this book

I am sure there are as many ways to use this book as there are people who read it. So please feel free to use it exactly how it feels right to you and your life. However, I'll enumerate a few possibilities for using it in the classroom as well as how the book is formatted to support you.

USING IT IN THE CLASSROOM

How you use the CLAIMING FACE curriculum in your classroom will largely depend on the time you have available, how much you want to engage in the philosophy behind it and what you intend to get out of using it.

I WANT TO CLAIM FACE AND MAKE THE CURRICULUM MY OWN

DEEP STUDY. For complete engagement, take time for yourself before taking this curriculum into class, perhaps during the summer when your schedule may be less rigid. Read everything and just let the information sit before starting. Play with the ideas about *presence* in your own life. Watch where your imagination wants to wander. Engage with the *Imagine* exercises and the *Reflect* questions. Visit an art store or even a drugstore; many have the basic art materials. Make yourself a starter kit of materials that interest you and choose a project. It could take you the whole summer to do all the projects or it could take you the whole year or even two. There is plenty of time. You will feel like sharing it with your students when it feels right. In fact, you won't be able to NOT share it at some point because you will have first hand experience of how it feels to claim your own face. Through this way you will come to your own knowing about the philosophy and most likely make the curriculum your own. **You will become the artist in the classroom.**

I WANT TO FOLLOW ALONG WITH MY STUDENTS

STUDY AS YOU GO. Let's say you want to bring the curriculum into the classroom immediately, but want to feel solid in the material. I would suggest reading all three parts, doing the *Imagine* exercises and *Reflect* questions, and then completing the projects progressively throughout the year, but a week or a few days before your students. In this way you'll be prepared for what they are about to do and speak from an immediate place of knowing about the experience.

I WANT TO SUPPORT MY STUDENTS

BE PRESENT. Perhaps you want to bring the curriculum into the classroom immediately but you can't pull off doing the projects beforehand in any way. No problem. Read the chapters, read the *Imagine* exercises and *Reflect* questions, take a glance at the *Cheat Sheet* on pg. 192, and show up. Your presence with them is vital whether or not you have done the exercises, answered the questions or completed any projects. Just be there.

I WANT TO USE IT RIGHT THIS MINUTE

IMMEDIATE SUPPORT. And finally, what if you get the book and you want to do the projects with your students right away. If you have paper and crayons,

ARTIST (n.)

Creativity is the teacher that lives within each of us. Being an artist means that no matter what activity we are engaged in, we are listening to and guided by our inner teacher.

some projects can begin immediately. Look at the *Materials* required for each of the projects and choose one that fits with what you have on hand.

Just like **RULE #2: *There is never a right or wrong way to make art,*** there is never a right or wrong way to begin working with CLAIMING FACE curriculum. Just begin. The only thing I ask you to bring with you are *THE 3 RULES*. *THE 3 RULES* above all else are the easiest way to bring the philosophy into the classroom. They provide the students with a structure to work in while also giving them room to expand and grow.

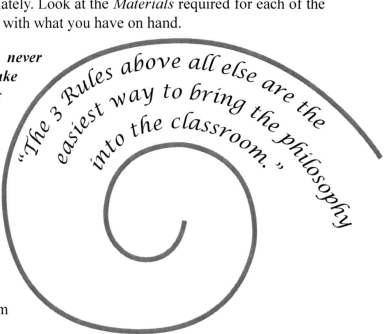

"The 3 Rules above all else are the easiest way to bring the philosophy into the classroom."

THE BOOK FORMAT

The format of the book is specifically designed for multiple ways of knowing the CLAIMING FACE curriculum. Whether you have plenty of time to engage in deeper study or are pressed for time and need a quick overview, you can use this book to your advantage.

THE LAYOUT

As mentioned previously, the book is divided into three parts. They are based on what specific experience we are engaging with. *Part One, Inside*, we engage with the philosophy and our internal experience. *Part Two, Outside*, we engage with setting up the physical space. And, in *Part Three, Process* we engage with the actual 26 CLAIMING FACE projects. Each Part is further divided into chapters.

IMAGINE & REFLECT. Following each chapter of *Part One*, and again at the end of *Parts Two* and *There*, are the *Imagine* exercises and the *Reflect* questions.

The *Imagine* exercises invite you to expand into and experience the philosophies and your physical presence from an internal position through your imagination. The exercises are designed to naturally lead you into taking up your pencil or pen and begin drawing. This builds the connection between creativity and your sense of self. There is space after each visualization to draw, doodle, sketch, or whatever calls you. You will also notice that any blank page in this book invites you to claim it as your own. Make your mark.

The *Reflect* questions provide the opportunity to explore your own thoughts, experiences and stories in relation to claiming your own face. This is your life, your work, your curriculum. Here is your chance to pause and take time to bring yourself into the moment more and more. Your presence is what is important.

KEYS TO REMEMBER. At the end of each chapter you will find the *Keys to Remember*. This summarizes the important points of the chapter to carry with you as you progress through the book. Just like the imagery of the keys in **Nana's Big Surprise**, they serve to help you unlock the potential power of this curriculum in your classroom. These *Keys* are also compiled at the end of the book into a *Claiming Face Cheat (Please!) Sheet*. Just like you'll find that I invite children to "cheat" when making art, I also invite you as well.

NANA'S BIG
SURPRISE

PROJECT PAGES. Additionally, each of the 26 CLAIMING FACE projects have been organized in a double spread format, shown on the following page (*pg.16*).

On the right page of the spread is everything you need to complete a project with your class (or with yourself): the *Purpose of the Project, Prep* (if any), *Materials, Books* (to add additional dimension to the project), and the actual *Process* to guide your students.

"It is valuable to acknowledge, make room for and engage with as many ways of knowing as possible."

The left page provides step-by-step photographs about the project to help you visually understand the different steps. While the photos are here to assist you, the projects in the photos have been intentionally left very simple to make room for your own (and your students') creative energy to rise up. The left page also offers you an opportunity to journal about your experience with the project: your own, your students, what you learned, what worked, what didn't, you can write anything here that will help you as you work with the projects in the future. It may even be that you decide to change the project to better suit your class. Or perhaps the project gave you ideas about other projects. Use this space for whatever you need. **Journal. Play. Explore. Discover and make your decisions as the artist in the classroom.**

It is valuable to acknowledge, make room for and engage with as many ways of knowing as possible. This expands not only your own experience and available ways to know, but allows you to understand that others come to their knowing in their own unique way. To this end, the guide provides the advantage of understanding through reading, experiencing through imagination, exploring through questions and engaging through projects. This encourages the most full assimilation of the CLAIMING FACE curriculum in order to support and empower you as an individual. From this position you can become a model in being and understanding for students to emulate in the classroom should you choose to share the work.

PROJECT PAGES EXPLAINED

Classroom Notes: Journal about your experience with the project; for yourself and in the classroom.

Project Symbols: Indicates what category the project is in and whether the project is part of the Fundamentals Schedule.

Classroom Notes:

What I learned from doing the project myself:

I learned that I still really love to cut & paste

Remember to bring the leftovers home to play with the kids!

What did or didn't work in the classroom:

It was easier to have everything already laid out when kids came in from recess.

Purpose of Project: Helps you mentally prepare for the project and connects philosophy with the project.

Project Name: Number refers to the project's place in the Full Schedule

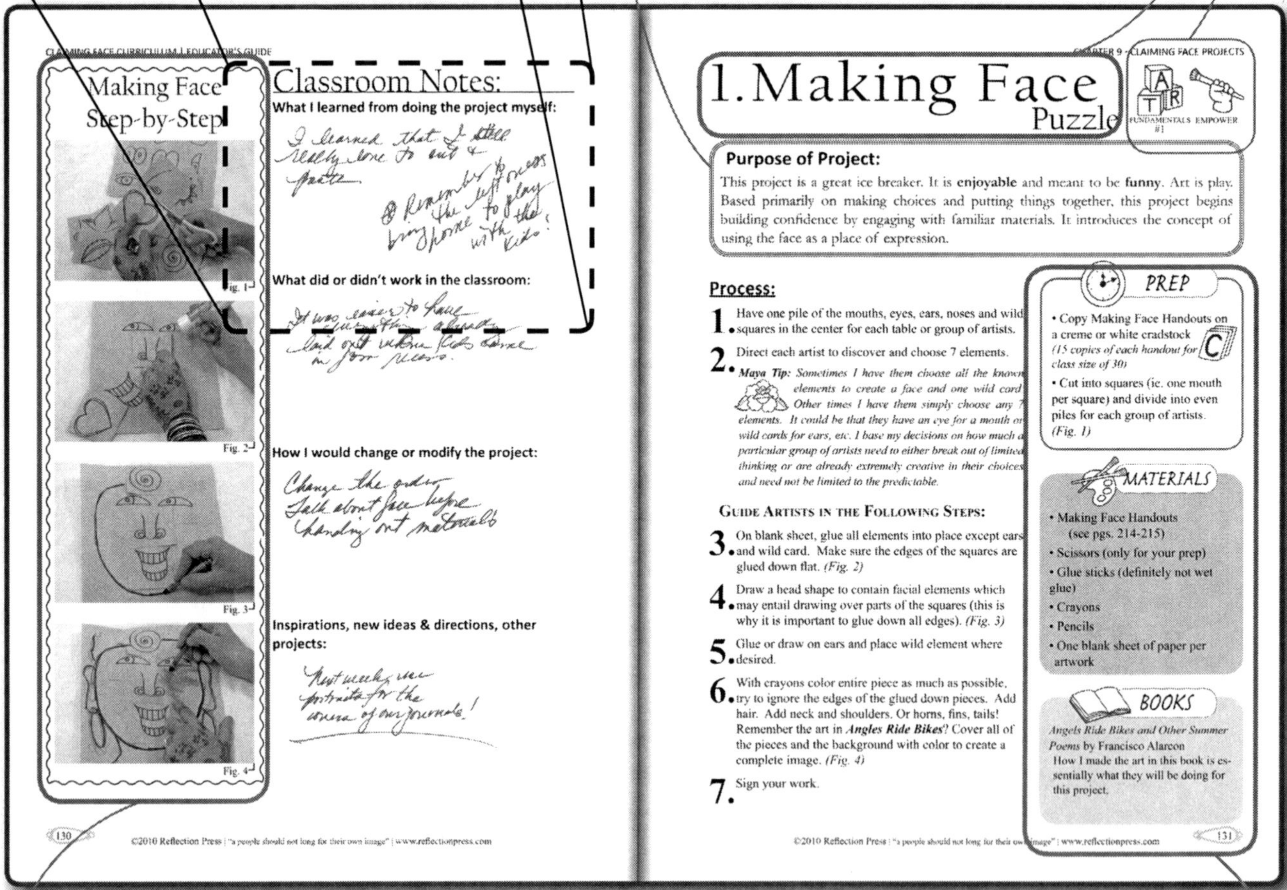

CLAIMING FACE CURRICULUM | EDUCATOR'S GUIDE

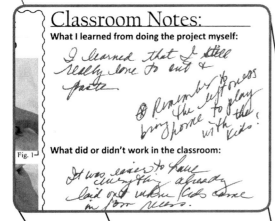

Making Face Step-by-Step

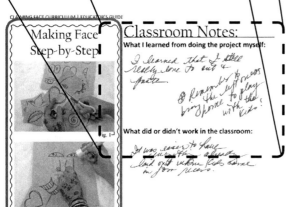

Fig. 1 Fig. 2 Fig. 3 Fig. 4

Classroom Notes:

What I learned from doing the project myself:

I learned that I still really love to cut & paste

Remember to bring the leftovers home to play with the kids!

What did or didn't work in the classroom:

It was easier to have everything already laid out when kids came in from recess.

How I would change or modify the project:

Change the order

Talk about face before handing out materials

Inspirations, new ideas & directions, other projects:

Next week use portraits for the covers of our journals!

130 ©2010 Reflection Press | "a people should not long for their own image" | www.reflectionpress.com

CHAPTER 9 - CLAIMING FACE PROJECTS

1. Making Face Puzzle

FUNDAMENTALS EMPOWER #1

Purpose of Project:

This project is a great ice breaker. It is **enjoyable** and meant to be **funny**. Art is play. Based primarily on making choices and putting things together, this project begins building confidence by engaging with familiar materials. It introduces the concept of using the face as a place of expression.

Process:

1. Have one pile of the mouths, eyes, ears, noses and wild squares in the center for each table or group of artists.
2. Direct each artist to discover and choose 7 elements.

Maya Tip: Sometimes I have them choose all the known elements to create a face and one wild card. Other times I have them simply choose any 7 elements. It could be that they have an eye for a mouth or wild cards for ears, etc. I base my decisions on how much a particular group of artists need to either break out of limited thinking or are already extremely creative in their choices and need not be limited to the predictable.

GUIDE ARTISTS IN THE FOLLOWING STEPS:

3. On blank sheet, glue all elements into place except ears and wild card. Make sure the edges of the squares are glued down flat. *(Fig. 2)*
4. Draw a head shape to contain facial elements which may entail drawing over parts of the squares (this is why it is important to glue down all edges). *(Fig. 3)*
5. Glue or draw on ears and place wild element where desired.
6. With crayons color entire piece as much as possible, try to ignore the edges of the glued down pieces. Add hair. Add neck and shoulders. Or horns, fins, tails! Remember the art in *Angels Ride Bikes*? Cover all of the pieces and the background with color to create a complete image. *(Fig. 4)*
7. Sign your work.

PREP

- Copy Making Face Handouts on a creme or white cradstock *(15 copies of each handout for class size of 30)*
- Cut into squares (ie. one mouth per square) and divide into even piles for each group of artists. *(Fig. 1)*

MATERIALS

- Making Face Handouts (see pgs. 214-215)
- Scissors (only for your prep)
- Glue sticks (definitely not wet glue)
- Crayons
- Pencils
- One blank sheet of paper per artwork

BOOKS

Angels Ride Bikes and Other Summer Poems by Francisco Alarcon

How I made the art in this book is essentially what they will be doing for this project.

©2010 Reflection Press | "a people should not long for their own image" | www.reflectionpress.com 131

Photos of Project Process: Figure number udner photo corresponds to steps of the process

Prep, Materials, Books: Prep: involved prep will have a PLUS sign next to the clock; watch for the camera and copy symbols. Materials: use Chapter 7 as a reference Books: Use Chapter 8 as a reference

THE SYMBOLS

In your exploration of the curriculum, you will notice various symbols throughout. These symbols provide you with an **at-a-glance reference to draw connections between different parts of the curriculum.** Some symbols relate to an action you will need to take for a project, such as the camera symbol indicating you will need photos of your students. Some symbols relate to another part of the book, for example the resource symbol that directs you to the *Resources* to find out more information about a particular topic. And then there are the category symbols at the core of the CLAIMING FACE curriculum. They connect philosophy, experience, and projects. All 26 CLAIMING FACE projects are **organized into 6 project categories,** noted by the symbol in the upper right corner of the project page.

These category symbols are also found throughout *Part One, Inside* and serve to connect the philosophy to the 6 project categories.

Familiarize yourself with the symbols and use them to their full advantage. For example, let's say you are looking for an empowering project to do with your students to nurture self-confidence. To determine an appropriate project, look on the project pages for the empower symbol (shown below). Additionally, you may want to search out this symbol in *Part One* to review the philosophies related to empowerment.

SYMBOLS LEGEND:

 The 3 Rules
distillation of the CLAIMING FACE curriculum

 Keys to Remember
find these at the end of every chapter that highlight important points

 Resource
text underneath this symbol tells you where to look in the *Resources*

 Fundamentals Schedule
identifies projects that are part of the shorter monthly schedule

 Project Prep Required
based on class size of 30; a PLUS sign indicates more involved prep

 Materials for Project
corresponds to *Using The Materials* in *Ch. 7*

 Books Associated with Project
corresponds to *Ch. 8, Books: Behind the Story*

 Photos of Students needed
corresponds to *Working with Photographs* in *Ch. 7*

 Copies needed
handouts, photos, etc. usually onto a heavy cardstock

 Maya Tip
tips, tricks, examples from my work in the classroom

Teacher Tip
tips to make the project run smoother

THE 6 PROJECT CATEGORIES:

 Reflection
allows children to see themselves clearly in their art

 Express
allows children to define themselves

 Explore
helps children search and find themselves in the world

 Empower
nurtures confidence in ability to create and encourages powerful reflections of one's self

 Expand
challenges children to explore beyond the norm

 Freedom
helps children to shake free of limited thinking

Process: Building the Link Between Creativity and a Sense of Self

We use the CLAIMING FACE projects to engage the creative process. They serve as a container to hold us while we explore and come to know ourselves. All of the projects are a form of self-portraiture which begins building the direct link between creativity and a sense of self. In order to create our own reflections we must pay attention to ourselves. We inadvertently invest in a foundation of presence and personal reflection by doing this. The more reflection and presence we create the more our sense of self can rise and gain perspective allowing us to see ourselves for who we really are.

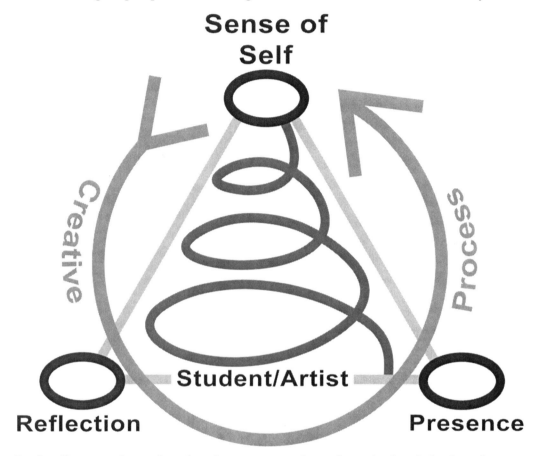

In the diagram above the triangle represents the artist, whether it is the educator or student. The flow of creative energy moves in a circle around the triangle symbolizing the container created when we engage with the projects and the creative process. The container, as well as the artist, is given weight and stability through the establishment of the base supplied by reflection and presence. This base supports a rising sense of self. **The dynamic effect these three elements, reflection, presence, and a sense of self, have on each other is represented by a triangle because the stronger and wider the base the more stable and elevated the top of the triangle becomes.**

In the following chapters reflection and presence will be explored through essays, exercises, questions, and practices to support building this base and prepare you to engage with the creative process through the projects.

On Teaching Art Skills

The curriculum is specifically not tied to teaching art skills. It is also not connected to other school subjects so that it can remain free and focused on the goal of connecting the creative process with a sense of self for the students. This allows the students to claim the curriculum as their own. However, many of the projects can and have been blended with other subjects by educators over the years. Reading, Math, Social Science, History, Science, Geography, Spanish, English, and more. My concern is not whether it is combined with other subjects or not, but that it support students in feeling a stronger sense of self which in turn helps students learn everything with greater ease and confidence.

I believe through my own experience and what I have witnessed in others that the stronger we feel in ourselves, the stronger we are in every aspect of our lives. When we have a strong sense of self it helps us to learn, make personally supportive choices, respect ourselves and those around us, and care about our lives and ultimately our world. CLAIMING FACE and claiming creativity will resource us as a people to create a world in which we are made stronger through genuine reflection, through knowing that we all belong here now, and through understanding our creative potential. This is our world.

I have made art with hundreds and hundreds of children over the years. Some of them stand out because they have taught me specific lessons, but I have been affected and changed by all of them. Our children are generous and brave. They are resilient and searching. Many of them are longing and don't even know it. One of my favorite projects is the *I Am Here Flags*. The students create hand portraits using oil pastels on a square of black cloth. Hands are the most basic and ancient form of self-portraiture. On the cloth there is an outline of their hand with drawing added and the words **I AM HERE** written along the bottom with their names. Once finished, the squares of cloth are gathered and connected to a long cord or ribbon and hung like small flags. The cord is then tied in the trees outside of their class where the students can see it. The flags are visually striking and as the wind catches them, they dance and shiver against the sky. Their beauty and intent riding the vibrations of the wind, sending out a message for each student:

I am here, I am here, I am here… Imagine…

Notes from 3rd graders about CLAIMING FACE:

Thank you for teaching me about art and that there is no right or wrong.
- Roberto

My favorite art was the self portraits. You showed me not to be afraid of my art to be bad. - Marcos

You showed me how to do the most fantastic art I've ever done. - Abel

I appreciate you because you got me into the art spirit. I used to hate art but now I like it! You've shown me the key to art.
- Ruben

You really got me into art a lot and now I be doing art at home. - Cargesha

Pause for a moment. Take your time. This is your life, your time. Each moment. Each thought and concern. Feel the weight of your body. Fill your place. It is yours. Notice your breath. Follow its path in and out, deep within and then up, up and out. Listen to it. It knows its path without thought. You can trust your breath. It is always a part of you.

We each have moments, experiences in our lives, some long, some short that hold some sorrow, some twinge of disappointment or pain. Even as children, there may be long sweeps of endurance and adjustment. Sometimes they are mixed back and forth, grief with happiness. There may be times of joy, close to exaltation, spontaneous and exuberant. It is the great energy of growing and exploring in a world that can only be new, even in the midst of challenge. **All things: an adventure. Courage, strength, resilience alongside uncertainty, shyness, fear**.

Lay your hand across your forehead. *Is it warm or cool? Do you recall passing through a fever as a child? How weak and how strong you were at the same time?* You are here now. No matter how high the fever, you passed through it. Something strong and insistent lived within you. It lives there still. *How does your face still carry this strength?* Use both hands to cradle your face. Touch your cheeks. *Are they full and round? Or high and hollow?* Touch your nose. *Is it wide and full or long and pointy?* Touch your lips. *Are they thick or thin? Do your eyes tip upward or downward or lay straight?* Feel the full of your face. *Is it round? Square? Long? Wide?* **Know your face.** Claim each nuance. It carries your story. It speaks of you before you do. *What does your face say? If you were to draw only one shape for your face, what would it be?* **Draw it, show yourself.**
Claim your face.

1 When you look at someone's face, what do you see? Facial features? Color? Expression?

Reflect

2 What kind of faces do you see the most? Are they the same as yours? What is similar? What is different?

3 When you look in the mirror, what does your face look like? What does your face convey without you saying a word?

4 What are 4 things about you that someone cannot know by looking at your face?

KEYS TO REMEMBER FROM CHAPTER 1:

- Our face communicates something about us that as children we may not understand.

- We sense that we belong and are valued in our culture when we see ourselves in the media in our world.

- Graffiti that impacted me: "a people should not long for their own image."

- I realized that if we don't want to long for our own image, we are going to have to create it for ourselves.

- CLAIMING FACE means to value ourselves for who we really are.

- The Educator's Guide is divided into three parts: *Inside*-development and philosophies, *Outside*-setting up the physical environment and *Process*-26 projects based on self-portraiture.

- The curriculum is for:
    - Anyone who is curious (you DO NOT have to consider yourself an artist or feel creative in any way).
    - Educators wishing to increase the cultural capacity of their class.
    - Educators wishing to empower their selves.
    - Educators wishing to empower their students.
    - Educators working with ESL students.

- You can choose how much time you want to work with the Guide from deep study to immediate support.

- The Guide is designed to be easy to use.

- Familiarize yourself with the different symbols to provide an at-a-glance reference to different parts of the curriculum (see Symbols Legend on page 17).

- The curriculum is not tied to teaching art skills, meeting standards or other academic subjects so that it can be personally claimed by each student.

- The CLAIMING FACE curriculum can be blended with academic subjects if so desired.

- Whether it is tied to other subjects or not, it will support students personally and academically.

CHAPTER 2

Through Creativity and
Deep Into Reflection

C reativity is the path in. Through it all things are possible. As the educator, begin by playing with the *Imagine* exercises and *Reflect* questions. Later, the projects will provide a way to engage with creativity. As you learn through the book, however, you will find that the enduring power of creativity is not found in what is created, but ultimately in the experience and act of creating itself: the process. The CLAIMING FACE curriculum leads us to use the power of creativity as a container to explore and empower while creating reflection. Reflection is a fundamental and necessary life experience. Its source and purpose may shift and evolve, but given time and attention, reflection and the act of reflecting deepens to encompass the layers and complexities that comprise who we are and what we live.

Over the next pages, I explore how reflecting on our self has meaning and contributes to empowering our self to live our best lives and how reflection is not exclusive to imagery. Through action we can create *Universal Reflection* and model and perpetuate new ways of being and thinking based on equality and courage. The act of reflecting on, or observing, is even now being "scientifically" understood to make an important impact on an experience. We affect what we observe.

The Power of Creativity

Is creativity important? What does it do for us? Is it important enough to have in our schools? How do you teach creativity?

Some people think that "creativity" is about art. When we think about it in school, we may frame it like other subjects, such as reading or writing. Teach the basics: technique and history. We may imagine Picasso or Da Vinci, or Michelangelo and call to mind the products of their work like the Mona Lisa or The Sistine Chapel. These men stand as icons, heroic and bigger than life, the epitome of "ARTIST." This can make art feel far away and inaccessible.

The truth is that creativity belongs to all of us.

When I was a child, I loved making things, all kinds of things. I also loved the beautiful and magical art in the Bible and dreamed about what it must have been like to be Michelangelo. I thought making art was different than the other things I made. There was something special about it. Unlike crocheting or sewing, making art always showed me something about myself. I remember drawing at 4 years old. I drew myself a lot. In search of reflection and not finding it, I created my own. Out of necessity, I took my love of making things, my own creative force and focused it on making art. This opened me up to pretend that I *was* Michelangelo.

"But the real power comes from being able to engage with our birthright and know how to use our creative power to serve us."

So when I teach creativity, I use art specifically. I could teach crocheting or knitting, sewing or jewelry-making or many other things I love to do. But I have found there really is something special about creating fine art. Artists through time have used it to honor, document, explore, express, imagine and more. It serves a special place for us as humans. We are all born creative beings. It is our birthright. And so is art. Art, even someone else's art is special because it shows us something about ourselves. It becomes even more personally relevant and powerful when we can claim our own creativity and make that art for ourselves. No one can show us ourselves more than ourselves.

Because we are born creative beings, childhood is naturally one of the most creative and spontaneous times in our lives. Most children make art of some kind. This makes childhood the perfect time to introduce art as a tool for self-awareness and empowerment, especially for our under-represented children, like children of color, whom I have primarily worked with. They are often in great need of meaningful reflection. I have seen that developing creativity goes a long way toward retaining or reclaiming the power we are born with. **It brings children back to themselves by their own hand.**

As such, the drawings and paintings we use as reflections to know ourselves are important, especially in the moment of creation. But as is life, these moments move. We change, we grow and go on. A drawing that seemed to teach us everything we needed to know one day must make room for the next drawing the next day. Drawings and paintings pile up; get misplaced, given away, even sold. What is left behind when the art is gone? Do we cease to know ourselves? Does the art that remains just pile up? Does a drawing still have meaning when we've moved on to the next piece?

Our art serves a number of purposes. First, it reflects and shows us ourselves in the moment, which is the most important part. Next it serves as a marker along the way of the creative process, a sign post on the road. It documents progress. And for that we are grateful because we can fill our world with our most current, beautiful and relevant reflections. But the real power comes from being able to engage with our birthright and know how to use our creative power to serve us. The enduring power is the experience and knowledge of the process, not the product.

Identifying as an artist and using the creative force is a way of perceiving life and all of our activities. **Creativity is ours.** It can open children up to the possibility in the unknown or unexpected, **making children more fluid, flexible and curious. Children learn to listen to themselves**, to trust and know themselves through the process, the ups and the downs, the making and fading of art. As adults they may stop using paints and pencils but somewhere inside they will always know that everything they do is creative. They will feel their own force and their ability. Hopefully they will even remember that in school they were taught *THE FIRST RULE*:

EVERYONE IS AN ARTIST!

The Importance of Reflection

When we see ourselves reflected in our environment, something happens within us. We are calmed, soothed, validated in a way that has no thoughts or words. An osmotic communication that we are, we belong. So fundamental that it goes without saying, it is about being. Being here now.

As a child I did not see myself reflected in the media which comprised my world. So I created my own reflection. As an adult, I now understand how important it was for me to see myself reflected in the world around me. Yet, as I have had the great privilege of creating so much imagery like this, I've found that I have not filled pages

REFLECTION (n.)
TO REFLECT (v.)

(1) An image outside of us that replicates either our actual image, as in a mirror or shows us something about ourselves, as in art, or the sunset. (2) To pause and focus one's attention in careful consideration on a thought or image.

with images of Chicanas solely because I needed to know that I exist. I have created images because I needed to know myself. I like the word reflection because of its double meaning. Reflection is an *image outside of us that replicates either our actual image, as in a mirror or shows us something about ourselves, as in art, or the sunset.* But also, reflection is *to pause and focus one's attention in careful consideration on a thought or image.* My personal work led me to link the two meanings. **I create reflections of myself so that I can reflect upon them to better know myself.**

Many of us are still not visible in the popular media. Our current culture creates media with the primary intent of selling, not necessarily documenting or reflecting our lives or telling children of color how strong and creative they are. In fact, because of the history of our culture, there is a dominance of white, middle-class, straight, male imagery. This leaves the majority of people in the world in a sense, invisible. This is not news. There are many people working hard to balance this, but I believe it is also important for us to acknowledge where things currently stand and create what change we can for ourselves now, in this moment. We are mobilized when we can accept that we are not reflected and take action. Through the CLAIMING FACE curriculum, students and educators alike create their own reflection to affirm presence, personal power, belonging and a deeper understanding of self.

Coming Face-to-Face with Myself

I have been going into public schools as an author/artist for many years. Initially when I went into the schools it felt that in the faces of the students, I was coming face to face with myself as a child. I was challenged to repeatedly see myself reflected in their faces. It reminded me of my own childhood, my own ghosts and haunts. As much as I wanted to distance from those memories, I realized this was part of my work as an artist. Facing them was indeed facing myself. At any point I could have said no, but I felt drawn to the faces and what lay within them. So I trusted and followed my draw to work with children, especially the ones who reflected me, the stressed out ones and children of color.

Maya, age 10

Now with an adult perspective, I can see and understand the underlying effects of invisibility and institutionalized racism, as well as the effects of living a layered and complicated childhood. This is what I experienced so I know firsthand how this erodes a sense of self and limits our curiosity, our ability to be independent and have our own thoughts. Although I was challenged in many ways as a child, I had art to negotiate the rocky terrain. When I began going into the schools to talk about being an artist for children's books, instead of talking about how to make a book and what it is like to be an illustrator I found myself sharing about how I used art as a child. Eventually, I began leading children in projects that mirrored what I had done and still do as an artist. As I evolved and matured as an artist and educator, I began to realize more and more the power of creativity. I understood how much it had supported me as a child and now I was seeing how it supported the children I worked with.

I still see myself in the students when I go into the schools and I'm happy for that!

As I have brought art and creativity into schools, I see that my lesson is their lesson and their lesson is mine. This is how the CLAIMING FACE philosophy and curriculum came into being. It is rooted in me and within every child with whom I have had the pleasure to work. I trusted that I belonged in schools working with children like myself.

Insight into Layered and Complex Reflection

In going into the classrooms, what I found was that many children are dealing with a comparable level of stress to what I was dealing with as a child. As an adult, I have more insight into my experience which in turn gave me insight into much of their experience. I STATISTICS grew up living in a high stress home like many of the children I work with. Creativity helped me carve out a space that was mine. It then served as a mediator between my internal experience and the larger realities in which I lived.

"Creativity helped me carve out a space that was mine. It then served as a mediator between my internal experience and the larger realities..."

 Although I identify as Chicana, I think it's important to also claim that I am biracial. This begins to acknowledge some of my complicated and layered reality, the stress that I experienced and the insight I gleaned. My life rises out of two powerful influences, both white and brown. My mother is white, my father Mexican. My mother and her side of the family were a strong presence when I was young. I find that as an adult however, I am more comfortable with my Mexican self. I feel more resonant with my father's side of the family, although my experience in relation to them was very intense. Intensity ran on both sides of my family, close family members both white and Mexican were emotionally unstable. Racial and cultural differences became embedded in another layer of experience and perception. When I look back I can't always tell what is having a greater impact: racial tension or emotional instability.

It's important to acknowledge the complications that children grow up with. I want to make it clear, I am an artist. I do not pretend to speak as a counselor or therapist. I speak solely from experience as someone who grew up with childhood stressors as well as being Chicana and biracial. To date, I have not gone into the schools and divulged what my personal experiences were. It's been sufficient to me so far that negotiating my experiences has influenced me and they inform what I teach. What I navigated as a child, what I know as an artist, and what I have learned as an educator is reflected in my perspectives on the creative process. I frame art as an important tool to negotiate multiple layers of understanding the self. This is what served me from age 4 until now. I trust that children will hold on to what serves them, when and how they need it, so

I have not felt the need to be explicit. But as I come forward to support educators, I want to share a brief overview of the nature of my history. It may give insight into how and why the CLAIMING FACE curriculum developed the way it did. Personally, in my immediate family, and with my extended family, I dealt with various aspects of the following while growing up: incest, emotional and mental instability, family dysfunction, alcoholism, divorce, serious physical injury, long term illness, death, direct and institutional racism, and homophobia.

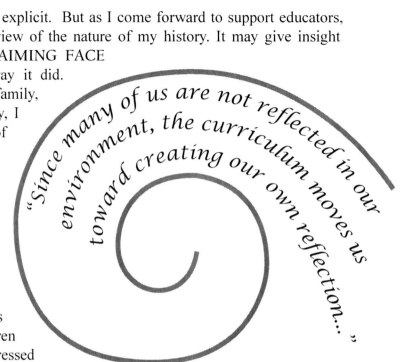

"since many of us are not reflected in our environment, the curriculum moves us toward creating our own reflection..."

STATISTICS

When I researched statistics for the various stressors children are dealing with, I was impressed with how much our children need not only more support, but specifically effective personal tools to hold onto for themselves. Creativity worked for me. I don't pretend that it will work for every child the way it has for me, but it will work for many and it will undeniably support all. Children who come from cultures that already value creativity may find it a natural fit. I believe that if we tacitly embed these tools into the basic classroom environment it will serve everyone in negotiating their personal lives, strengthening their curiosity and desire to learn, and negotiating school's social settings.

Reflection and the Witness Effect

CLAIMING FACE begins with the importance of seeing our self in our environment through reflection. Since many of us are not reflected in our environment, the curriculum moves us toward creating our own reflection to affirm our existence, belonging, and to create a reflection upon which to reflect as a tool to know our self. This is done through being present with our self. We are seeing or "witnessing" our self as we create art.

PRESENCE

Body psychotherapist, John Waterstone says about witnessing:

"In existential terms the fact of being seen is essential to the process of existence. The individual exists, i.e. stands out via the dynamic process of showing the self to the self and to others. The self is defined (comes into being) [...] by being /doing in the eyes of another, in the eyes of the self, and in the witnessing of the impact of the self on the other."

Witnessing is the "dynamic process" that occurs. Something happens when we are present with our self or another. **We change things by observing them.**

Scott Jeffrey, theorist and author, says:

"When you witness something, it changes. At the quantum level, the choices you make—your intention—shifts the probability of a potentiality..."

This dates back as long ago as the 1927 Copenhagen Solvay Conference which concluded that: **the observer and that which is observed are inextricably linked and must not be viewed as separate.**

QUANTUM
PHYSICS

Through witnessing ourselves and others, especially while making art about ourselves, we can affect invisibility and the unspoken messages that go with it.

We have a need to be seen. It begins when we're babies looking up into our parent's eyes. It is the first time we are seen. Through this we become. From the beginning being seen connotes connection at a fundamental, existential level. In contrast, not being seen, being invisible can render us insignificant, possibly isolated and communicates unspoken volumes to our deepest self.

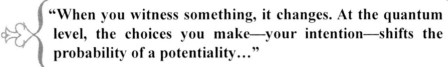

"Through witnessing ourselves and others, especially while making art, we can affect invisibility and the unspoken messages that go with it."

As we develop it is possible and sometimes necessary to relocate our source of who sees us to the inside. When we move "who sees us" inside. We see ourselves. We are our own witness. This internal seeing is so fruitful that it has been used as a meditative practice for over 5000 years in some cultures. Ironically, over the last 90 years, Quantum Physics is beginning to slowly formulize the profound effects of seeing or "witnessing" and being witnessed into scientific theory. This could ultimately shift the way we perceive reality and our effect on it. Witnessing is a strong, structural support embedded in the curriculum through the importance of reflection, the practice of presence, and the format of the projects focused on knowing self.

WITNESS (n.)

A person who sees and pays close attention to either one's self or another. Witnessing strengthens the vitality of existence and presence of the one who is seen and has an effect on who is seen in accordance with intent. For example, if the seer's intent is to respect who they are seeing, then respect will become a relational factor.

For years I have guided children to make reflections of their selves. I love looking at their work, their wonderful amazing child drawings, immediate and fresh. But what strikes me most is the sound of their voice and the look in their eyes when they show me. They are excited to investigate who they are and generous in wanting to show me every detail. It's as if for a moment I am watching them become more themselves.

Universal Reflection

Reflection obviously conveys something very deep and important. It supports children to sense their belonging and can give vision to who they are and what they can become. This is valuable to all children, but especially children of color who are generally under-represented. When I go into schools, I know part of my job is to just be there and show that Chicanas who grew up working class, out in the middle of the desert can be artists, authors, and educators. As such, we can tell our stories, we can reflect our community and we can affect our world.

When I am in the classroom, I reflect who students can become. When I am not there, my books serve as reflection. But CLAIMING FACE is not about me or my books; it's about the creative process. Through sharing the creative process I found I could more easily perceive a deeper equality between me and the students. We were fundamentally all doing the same work, coming to know ourselves and facing our individual unknowns. The process was the same. We were all CLAIMING FACE. The only thing that was different was *what* we were learning. But even this was the same in that it was relevant to where each of us was in our lives. I call this *Universal Reflection*. It is not a visual reflection. It is a reflection through action and it is available between everyone. Naturally, my experience in the classroom deepened as I understood that not only were the students my reflection as I shared earlier, they were my equals. I could see this most clearly in the fact that they taught me as I taught them. It was circular.

This is one of the reasons I encourage educators to engage with the CLAIMING FACE curriculum as much as possible for themselves. This is an opportunity to dismantle subtle and pervasive power structures that promote inequality in our current culture between child and adult, between white people and people of color, between educator and student, between men and women and so on. Not only will you see yourself and your students as more and more equal, but also through engaging with the same work, your students will see themselves in you, the educator. Each of you facing your individual unknowns and your inexperience about what you're doing, learning how to create your own reflection, and coming to know yourselves through experience and the art you create. It is powerful when students see their process and work reflected and equal to their educator's. **The CLAIMING FACE curriculum expands the possibilities for reflection and unifies us through our shared birthright, Creativity.**

Take a moment to feel your body resting on your seat. Your full weight pulling you down to your place on the Earth, like a stone resting on the ground, solid and full. This place where your body rests is yours. No one else can fill it. You are here. Now. Notice your breathing, in and out. You are solid, but you are not dense. Feel your chest opening up to take in your breath and your chest resting down to let it out. Follow your breath for a moment into your body through your lungs and then out into the air around you. Naturally, without effort you begin again. Breathing. In this moment now, everyone is breathing this air that surrounds our planet. We are all breathing.

You may now be in your 20's, 30's, 40's, 50's 60's, 70's.... Feel your age, the wisdom that you have gathered, the experiences, feelings, relationships. You have been breathing all this time. Always in and always out. Follow your breath for a moment back to your childhood. After a hard run, rising from a nap, blowing out a candle on a cake.

Imagine you are holding your favorite book. Its pages are smooth and cool in your hand. Look. *What do you see on the page? Do you see a face there like your own? Can you enter that face, enter that story as if it were your own? Is it familiar? Does it mirror your life?* Many of us didn't see our face or our lives reflected in the books we grew up with. Look at the book in your hands. *Is your face there?* If it isn't, using your powerful imagination, feel yourself as a child holding a book and looking down you see a face that looks like you and you can read a story that sounds just like your life.

Now as a child look up and out into your world, do you see your face in the movies that you watch, the billboards in your town, the newspapers, magazines, television programs? Do you hear songs on the radio about wise children, strong girls, the perfection of brown skin warming in the sun? What is on the nightly news? What kind of stories and images filled the background of your childhood?

And what about your hands? Do they hold crayons? Brushes dipped in watercolors? Thick sidewalk chalk? What about mud? What about glue bottles?

Look at the hands you have now. *What wisdom do they still carry from childhood?* Do not think thoughts. Allow your wise hands to move. Touch a pencil to this page. Scribble. Draw. One letter. *The first letter you ever made?* **Begin. Begin here with yourself. You are an artist. There is never a right or wrong way to make art.**

Use the following page to draw whatever calls to you........

Draw it! Claim it!

Draw it! Claim it!

Draw it! Claim it!

Reflect

1. Did you grow up with media that you feel reflected you and your life? What kind of media did you grow up with? What was in the books? On the radio? On the nightly news? In the movies and on the television?

2. When you look around your world today, do you see yourself reflected in your world? How many people who hold power in our current culture look like you? Have a similar story as yours?

3. When you imagine being fully reflected in your world, how do you feel? Is it different or the same as how you felt as a child? How about now? Do you feel fully reflected in your world now? Imagine for a moment that you do.

4. When you feel fully reflected in your world, how does that affect your learning? Your ability to assimilate information?

5. When you imagine that you are fully reflected in your world, is it the same world? Does it feel different? Is the information available the same? Are the social, economic, spiritual, mental, physical values the same? If they're different, how?

KEYS TO REMEMBER FROM CHAPTER 2:

• The real power of creativity is being able to use it to empower our self, for example through creating our own reflection.

• When we are reflected in our world, we sense that we belong.

• Creating reflections of ourselves allows us to reflect upon and better know ourselves.

• It's valuable to understand the underlying effects of invisibility and institutionalized racism.

• Witnessing is the dynamic process that occurs when we are seen by another or by our self.

• We change things by observing them.

• *Universal Reflection*: reflection becomes universal when it is not dependent on image but on action between two or more people.

• Creating reflection through action equalizes student and educator and helps to dismantle and balance power structures that exist in our current culture.

• When you engage with the curriculum for yourself:
   - You create your own reflection
   - You come to know yourself more deeply
   - You provide *Universal Reflection* for your students
   - You demonstrate the equality between you and your students
   - You serve as a model to witness and emulate
   - You learn, you grow, bigger, stronger, you become even more fabulous!

CHAPTER 3

Energy and Presence

There is an Eastern saying, *"The teacher and the taught together create the teaching."* I teach what I know and what made a difference in my life. Understanding the flow of energy and working with presence or "witnessing" has been an ever-deepening aspect of the creative process that I feel has lightened my load. I used to use my brain to think everything out and be confused when I couldn't cognize the answers. Now I find that I have access to greater wisdom and creative flow if I drop into the moment by paying attention to the here and now. Using presence with the curriculum gives more weight to the process and enhances the effect of the projects. A kind of synergy occurs between creating reflection, witnessing yourself and being present. When we are present as educators, first with ourselves and then with our students, something occurs; something changes.

In this chapter, I explore the nature of energy and the effects of presence on it. This lays the framework for the following chapter, *Presence in Practice*, where I ground how to practice presence in your life, your interactions with your students and in your classroom to derive the most benefit from the CLAIMING FACE curriculum.

Chaos, Control, and The Flow of Energy

Studies show that the majority of adults have a 4th grade level of creativity. So it is probably safe to say that most of us have not been exposed to creativity much. We probably don't know a lot about our own creative potential and may see ARTISTS as someone else. It makes sense that creativity and its flow could feel unfamiliar, even dangerous and overwhelming to some. I have had teachers imagine that if their students had the freedom to fully express themselves they would run amok, even destroy things. When creative energy is perceived like this it can seem like something that must be controlled or chaos will ensue.

This fascinates me, but it makes perfect sense. Change, even supportive, positive change can bring confusion. Can we handle the energy? Will it be too much for us? What if we have a classroom full of fully empowered children completely free to express their whole and true selves? What will happen?

 Creative energy can feel big at times and some children, given the freedom to really express themselves have a lot of energy to move through them. **However, the curriculum is designed to support freedom coming up slowly over time so the energy and our ability to hold it can build steadily.** The other primary support is the practice of presence. **Presence is fundamental to the CLAIMING FACE curriculum and is a primary tool for dealing with energy of all kinds.** It's important to let steam off regularly. If there is a lot of energy building up, don't push it down. Let it move, while working within the respectful boundaries of your classroom, of course. I have a playful trick I like to use that illustrates how the movement of energy can be guided to flow while contained.

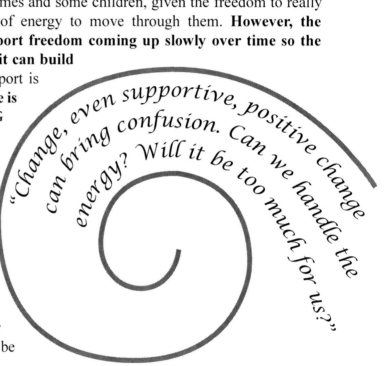

"Change, even supportive, positive change can bring confusion. Can we handle the energy? Will it be too much for us?"

THE BOB TRICK

 I often have large numbers of students after recess or lunch. There's a lot of energy moving through their bodies. That's when I use my "Bob Trick." You may not be able to do exactly this in your classroom, perhaps you can do it outside or concoct your own "quieter" version with similar results. I tell the students that my legal name is Maya Christina Deriu Smith-Gonzalez, a noticeably long name, even Maya Christina is a bit long. So, if they must, they can call me "Bob!" I then ask them to join me in yelling "Bob" as loud as possible. At first this surprises them. Yelling is seldom acceptable at school, but it doesn't take long before there is an amazing chorus of BOOOOOOOOOOOBBBBB ringing out. I tell them that we must get all of the "Bob" up and out. Once started no "Bob" can be left in their bodies. This may take a couple of good yells. It definitely takes a moment to quiet down, but that is worth it to me. Not only because I trust the rising and falling of energy, but because once the energy moves up and out, it is actually easier for the students to stay focused. A practice like this demonstrates that energy can come up, even in a strong and loud way and come back down again. It is not dangerous. No one was hurt. No one was out of control. In fact, because there was a clear and firm form held by me, the energy can rise and then land within the container I am holding with the exercise. I always create a physical "ending" action, like raising both arms to show we've gotten all the Bob out. The "landed" energy is more centered. The "Bob Trick" is comparable to art. They both can serve as containers for energy to come up and move through while being held.

During these experiences, I often notice that the educators seem uncomfortable. In my imagination, I wonder if the energy seems out of control to them and it's their job to keep everyone quiet. Few join in the yell. I've seen some fidget or stand up unexpectedly. But I notice, once "Bob" has moved through, both the educators and students tend to settle in more fully and listen and engage more. Energy naturally rises and naturally falls. It does not need to be pushed down. In fact, in pushing it down, children often have a harder time focusing. This is important to pay attention to. We want energy to flow. This is basic to creativity. The more we can free our energy to flow, the more expressive we can be. This allows us to explore creativity more, which means we can know ourselves more. This is essential on the path to empowerment.

"The curriculum is designed to support freedom coming up slowly over time so the energy and our ability to hold it can build steadily."

I love it later when the students call me Bob. We always laugh because they know I was playing with them and they are in on the joke.

REBEL!

I believe it is important for children to know that we are advocates. We are on their side. Joking is a very good way. It gives the sense that we are "in on" something together. Doing something "risky" together is also effective.

I try to give students the opportunity and permission to do what "seems" like something they are not supposed to do. I create situations where they are supposed to "cheat" or draw the weirdest or scariest thing about themselves that no one can see. In a

FREEDOM (n.)

(1) The power to exercise choice and make decisions without constraint from within or without. (2) To allow an unencumbered flow of energy to move through one's self and life.

sense, I am giving them permission to do the "forbidden," in a very light way. It reminds us that art doesn't have to be "pretty," just real. Children are communicated to all the time about what is considered right or wrong, good or bad, real or not real, valued or devalued in our culture. By 4th grade our children are strongly affected by our overall paradigm; a paradigm that does not always include them. It is the constant and subtle messages that get in the deepest. For example, I bring up the issue of invisibility consistently because the CLAIMING FACE curriculum is specifically a response to it. Developmentally, a child isn't able yet to contextualize the world at large and the reality of their situation in it. Their lack of representation then serves as a backdrop. They are rendered invisible and yet their invisibility is just as invisible because it is simply perceived as "life." This conveys deep albeit subtle messages about worth, belonging and possibility. Making one's self visible changes the world as we know it and can be seen as a revolutionary or radical act.

When we "cross the line" and do something "we're not supposed to do," we personally dismantle some of the limiting judgments that have been placed on something like creativity. This creates a new pattern of thought. A pattern of making judgment visible and removing external influences helps us come to our own conclusions and understandings, especially about our self. Some children experience a great deal of judgment and energetic repression. I find these children need to get their wild side up and out for awhile. So it's beneficial to do "Freeing" projects regularly. Being free or even the promise of freedom can release a lot of energy. But as we are learning, energy given full expression comes back down again and settles into a more stable pattern. Generally once you get used to feeling free, you have a lot more energy freely flowing. The more your creative energy flows the more available it is to do with as you need.

Sometimes We Flow and Sometimes Not

I have studied mindfulness; worked with somatic therapy; and studied the nature of reality and Quantum Physics for many years. All of these influences have at their core: **presence, trust, freedom and creativity**. These have become fundamental to me when using art as a tool to know self. I've worked with creativity for so long; I can literally feel the energy of it moving through me. It can feel like something pulling on me, until I release into it. Once fully engaged I can either feel in full and effortless flow with the creative force or feel unsure and have to trust and suspend judgment.

TO TRUST (v.)

to relax into ourselves, the moment, and our lives and know that we can listen to ourselves and always find our way.

Sometimes things may come out hideous. But I trust that there is still something for me to know about myself in the hideousness. I learn and go on creating. Creativity is an unceasing teacher. For one, I have learned that nothing is "hideous."

Creativity is different all the time. Sometimes in the moment that I'm creating, I can think of nothing else, I'm keenly focused on the act of creating alone. There's a kind of peace. Other times, I have room to think many thoughts, usually very specific thoughts. I work out the details and shapes of my life during these moments. Still other times emotions come up and move through, sometimes without clear stories attached to them. Often, they're tied to the image I'm working on. I don't always understand what my images are showing me, sometimes for years. But inevitably if I look back I can see the connections and the directions in my art and how they reflect my decisions, choices, and intentions of that time. I can see how everything fit perfectly together to this end or that. I am still moved by the fact that I can make art about what I don't yet know or understand about myself and my life. That is the power of creativity and reflection.

"By 4th grade our children are strongly affected by our overall paradigm, a paradigm that does not always include them."

I have seen all of this in action with children. I've seen children so involved in their creating that nothing else matters. They are without thoughts. They are pure being in action. Other times I've seen children processing some aspect of their life while making art. It is as if the time they get to make art provides them with enough space to ponder and be present with something in their life and figure it out or let it move through them. I have also seen many children convinced that they've made something truly hideous come to understand that it is one of the most amazing pieces of art they have ever created.

How does creativity work for you?

In taking time to focus our attention inward, instead of compulsively outward (using art as a tool) we expand our awareness of the present moment and create room to experience more through art. This includes paying attention to energy in the body. I have had students and adults alike tighten up, even freeze up when creating art. I've seen it happen in body and in words. Often we're not used to noticing the energy in our bodies and it can feel like a giant wall. It may translate into words like "*I can't*" or "*this is too hard*" or even "*I'm bored.*" We don't have to spend our time trying to figure out what "the wall" is all about. As soon as you need to know what is moving through or blocking you, you'll know, because it is a part of you. Initially, just notice it and do not judge it. Let that energy be there. Tight or loose or cold or hot or spidery or prickly or just words. Notice it while you make art. You can even pay attention to the fact that all you hear in your head while you're making art is "*I can't. I can't. I can't.*" That's OK. Art is the container to hold you. It allows you to slow down, feel your body, know your thoughts, all while creating a reflection.

PAYING ATTENTION TO ENERGY FLOW

Witnessing, paying attention or being present are all ways to support the flow of energy. Energy comes in many different forms, physical, creative and emotional. Emotions rise and fall much like creative or even physical energy. An emotion is not an end product. Like art, it is a process. It helps to understand that all of our different kinds of energy are connected or related to each other in some way. Like physical and creative energy, emotional energy is meant to flow. Often our energetic patterns in one area of our life, affect our energy in other areas. If we suppress our physical energy it could result in our emotional energy overflowing. Or we suppress our creative energy which in turn suppresses our physical energy. In all areas, it is about not pushing something down, but allowing it to be there. In the most basic sense, if we notice something and give it room to move, it will. This will support us in transforming our energetic blocks in all areas of our life to move more strongly, smoothly and steadily.

PRESENCE

"Even more powerful is to know how to deal with stuck energy and how to harness it when it is free flowing for our empowerment."

Through long-term personal study as well as working with hundreds of children and adults, I have learned a great deal about energy. It is now clearer to me when it is stuck and easier for me to understand how to help it return to its natural motion. It is a powerful resource to recognize how energy behaves. Even more powerful is to know how to deal with stuck energy and how to harness it when it is free flowing for our greatest empowerment.

ENERGY (n.)

the creative force, the momentum within ALL things. Energy can transform, but it cannot be created or destroyed. It is constant. Quantum Physics is beginning to show us that EVERYTHING at the most fundamental level is made up of energy.

Energy is all around us and moving through us, but it can seem invisible if you're not used to paying attention to it. I have worked with creative energy for so long it's very familiar to me so I can see it and feel it very clearly. But for many years I needed a reflection outside of myself to understand emotional energy and how it related to creative energy for me. I paid attention to water. If water stands in one place for too long, it can stagnate. If water is allowed to build up without an outlet it will spill over and go anywhere it can, like filling a glass of water too full. If there's nothing underneath to catch it, the water will spill over without direction. If water moves through a channel it can clear out debris blocking its path and be directed to a specific end. Most importantly I noticed that energy moves in a wave pattern like water, rising, peaking, ebbing, and flowing.

The more you pay attention to water or whatever you're using as your metaphor for energy, the more you will understand the overall nature of energy and how it moves. This will naturally enhance your ability to "see" energy including your own and recognize when it is or isn't flowing in all ways. But if we recognize it and note that it is not flowing, how can we support it moving? Ironically, you've already begun. In being able to see something, you are beginning to pay attention to it. When you pay attention to something, it changes. Paying attention to something is what presence is all about.

Maya, from the book Just Like Me

Begin by Being Yourself

"You teach some by what you say, teach more by what you do, but above all, you teach most by who you are."

I know that children like it when I visit their school. It can feel like a party. But more than what I say or share or show, is who I am. Not who I am like: I'm **MAYA GONZALEZ, CHILDREN'S BOOK ARTIST AND AUTHOR**. No, not that! Because ultimately that isn't much, is it? When I get notes or letters, I hear a bit about what I said or did, but surprisingly I hear more about *"what kind of person I am"* and *"how that shows."* I blame creativity. Using it as a tool to know myself has forced me to really know myself. I can't hide much from myself so I don't have much to hide from anyone else. My good and strong and beautiful along with my eccentric, weird, and sometimes scary is all there. I'm not a walking tale of myself; I'm actually a bit private and shy about most of my stories. It's more of a silent communication that has to do with how I hold my body, the way that I speak, how I feel about myself, and how I move about the world. It's not that I do it perfect and pretty either, that's not the point. I have my own, terribly idiosyncratic way. I am myself. Authentic. That's honesty. And as we know, children can smell honesty!

"As an educator being yourself and letting the children see you be that way has an enormous effect."

41

As an educator being yourself and letting the children see you be that way has an enormous effect. You don't have to bare your soul or tell too many tales. It's more about being and letting them see you being. I encourage educators to do the projects first because I want you to feel empowered. I want you to pay attention to yourself. Feel that you belong. I want you to be here. That's an amazing role model. That's better than Michelangelo or Leonardo Da Vinci in my opinion. Just be. Let the children see you struggle with your own creative expression and courage, see you feel mad sometimes or exhilarated at what worked or struggling with courage at what didn't work out in your project. It gives them permission and a model to do the same.

 I like to pretend that *THE 3 RULES* are RULES. I also like to pretend that they have everything to do with art. But the truth is they only have to do with being. Herein lies our presence. No art is necessary. Art is just a container. I used to think I had to DO this, DO that, DO everything, DO anything until I figured out that all I really have to do is BE. Be an artist. Be me. In Being, I find that I accomplish everything that is important and often more and in better ways with a lot more peace. Everything begins with being yourself.

The Origin of Change

In the diagram to the right, self is at the center of an expanding spiral of effect reaching out wider and eventually to the world. This is how energy vibrates out, like a ripple effect through water. Empower yourself first. Know who you are outside of external definitions.

Paying attention to yourself and being more engaged with your own creative power is where change originates. Through this you will be being more of who you are. Even the smallest steps are valuable. A further benefit is that your students will witness you doing this. Your model will show them what it looks like, how it feels and how to do it. You will support and inspire through being yourself.

I wonder what teachers would teach if there were no standards to abide by; or if the most highly valued qualities in our culture were being creative and empowered? I wonder what students would learn in a world like that? All we have to do is begin with ourselves. The children will see it and be affected. They will take their experience out to their families and so on. **When we change, we change everything.**

Feel free to remind yourself:

You don't have to <u>DO</u> anything, you just have to <u>BE</u>. In that, is the strongest DOING there is. This is the power of *presence*.

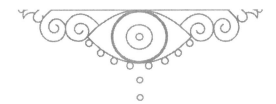

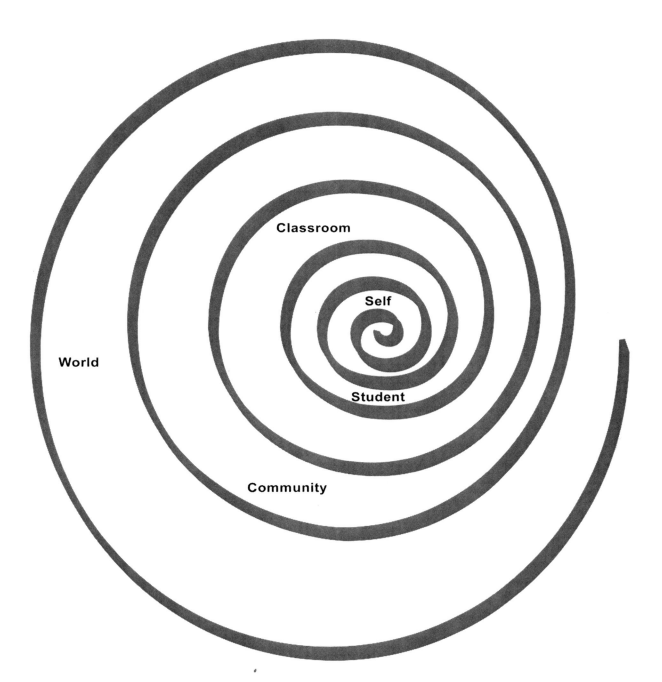

<u>The Origin of Change Spiral</u> - *self is at the center of an expanding spiral of effect reaching out wider and eventually to the world. This is how energy vibrates out, like a ripple effect through water. Empower yourself first. Know who you are outside of external definitions.*

Imagine Energy Flowing

Breathe. One, two, three. Notice your feet. Your weight. Think of a circuit for a moment. Something round. There is no beginning and there is no end. Just a constant, steady motion, round and around. It goes without effort, round.

And now it grows one step larger. Round and around. And one step more round and around. Not big steps. Natural steps. Another one, round and another. There is a pattern of growth, of flow, of expansion. Notice it reaching out. Now remember your breath. One, two, three. Your weight. You are the center that holds the core of this expansion. Simple, easy. Just notice. You don't have to do anything. Purposefully don't do anything. Just notice. Round.

What is the feeling or image of this circuit? Is it water? Is it electricity? Is it wind? A wheel? Is it a great machine? The cycle of life? Only you know. What is it that moves through you? Draw a circle. Go over and over the line. Feel how effortless this can be. Round and round. It's like it's drawing itself.

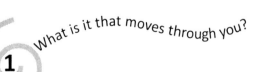

1 What is it that moves through you?

Draw it! Claim it!

Reflect

2 How does the energy inside your body move? Strong? Soft? Sporadic? Limited? Waves? Storms? Don't know?

Have there been times in your life when the energy in your body moves more strongly than other times? What happens when this energy moves in a strong way? Is there a limit? **3**

4 How does it feel when the energy in your body moves in a weak way? What energy flow feels the most comfortable to you?

Do you ever push your energy down? How do you do that? What other ways do you imagine energy could be pushed down? Do you feel there are times when you must push your energy down? **5**

6 If you were fully energized what would that feel like? How would that affect your sense of self? Your life? Your relationships? Your work? Your play?

KEYS TO REMEMBER FROM CHAPTER 3:

- The curriculum is designed to support freedom coming up slowly over time so that energy and our ability to hold it can build steadily.

- Being "in on something" with the children, like a joke, for example the "Bob" Trick, or taking a "risk" together, for example drawing something you're "not supposed to," is a way to show that you as the educator are on their side.

- Presence is fundamental to the CLAIMING FACE curriculum and is a primary tool for dealing with energy of all kinds.

- Don't push energy down. We want it to flow.

- Energy, whether creative, emotional, physical, or other, naturally rises and naturally falls.

- I use water as a metaphor to understand the nature of energy and how it moves.

- The purpose of some of the projects is to make judgment visible and help remove external influences in order to come to our own conclusions and understandings about our self.

- The most powerful thing you can do as an educator is be yourself.

- When we change, we change everything.

CHAPTER 4

Presence in Practice:
with Yourself, with Your Students, In the Classroom

*T*he CLAIMING FACE curriculum is rooted in presence. ***I am here. I belong.*** Statements like these resonate throughout the philosophies and the projects and are supported by ***THE 3 RULES*** and much more. It is one thing to understand the concept. What counts is being able to put it into practice, to experiment with and fathom the meaning for yourself. What is presence? I'm here. What more is there? How do you do it? What does it mean to bring it into the classroom? In this chapter, I explore the meaning of presence and how to work with it. Like in *The Origin of Change Spiral* on page 43, in this chapter, I discuss presence step by step: first with the self, which then extends out with the student, and then with the classroom. This is a very basic introduction. There is a lifetime of resources and experiences to be had, but it's worthwhile to bring it into the classroom and your life in even the most basic way. Art and creativity are great roads in. They are inextricably linked with presence.

The Rewards of Presence

I will never forget working with one particular boy. He was clearly dealing with a great deal of stress on every level of his life. I worked with his class every month for a year. This occurred a visit or two in. The class was beginning a project I had just laid out when I came by his desk. He just sat there staring at his paper and repeating,

"I can't. I can't. I can't." For a moment I was simply stunned and saddened. Until I realized, I understood what he was feeling.

Maybe our specifics were different, but the fundamentals were the same. Stressed, overwhelmed, defeated, lost, frozen. His sense of spontaneity and curiosity were already long gone. This made sense to me from some of my own experiences as a child. These are signs of long term stress. Without thinking about what I should do or could do, I just stopped and knelt down at his desk. The other 29 students vanished briefly as I completely noticed what he was experiencing. I noticed how he was sitting, the look on his face, his hands, and the sound of his voice.

After a moment in this expanded presence, I said for the first time, *ART IS ALWAYS AN ACT OF COURAGE.* Paying attention to his experience, coupled with making room for both fear and courage seemed to have a strongly supportive effect. Something lifted off of him. His hard feelings didn't "magically" disappear, but there was a distinct shift. He visibly changed. After a few minutes it appeared that he had more room for what he was experiencing as he gathered enough strength to move on. Not only did he finish that project, but his art continued to come through with power. I watched him change more over the course of that year. It seemed that something kept moving so that something else could keep coming forward. I wondered if he was like me. Art could always get in when nothing else could. Or maybe it was more the fact that I had stopped and was fully present with him. I was so struck by his response that *ART IS ALWAYS AN ACT OF COURAGE* became my *3RD RULE.*

PRESENCE

"I believe presence has been one of the main reasons as to why I have had such moving and powerful experiences with children…"

What Does Being Present Mean

PRESENCE

Except in specific circles, being present is not modeled or taught. In fact, it's so foreign to us that it can be challenging to explain. I discovered the lesson of being present embedded in my experience as an artist. I think because of my own history as a stressed out child, art served to help me not only express but also helped me be more present. As an adult, I worked with a practitioner who slowly trained me to be more and more present with myself. This made a noticeable difference in my life and gave me insight into how art and creativity had served me in this regard since I was a child.

Because I saw myself reflected in the children I worked with, presence naturally became an integral part of what and how I shared. I believe presence has been one of the main contributing reasons as to why I have had such moving and powerful experiences with children over the years, like the boy in the story. Children have confirmed for me what a difference it can make.

While I share some of what has been the most effective for me in working with children, I know that different things work for different people. I am sharing my experience as a guideline and support as you find what ways to be present work best for you.

To begin, let's acknowledge that **we all have all of the feelings, including stress, children and adults alike.** We all have bodies and it is here that our feelings are expressed. **Being present means that we're aware of our self as much as possible, especially our body.**

Take a moment to pay full attention to yourself, let everything else fade back. At first this could seem unrealistic or selfish or even uncomfortable. But it takes little time and can have a significant effect. I always remind myself of the *"oxygen-mask-rule."* That piece of advice flight attendants give you during the safety demonstrations before an airplane takes off. They tell you to put your own mask on, then put your child's mask on. This is the "safest." **We are most effective when we attend to our selves first.**

PRESENCE

BEGIN WITH YOURSELF

I found that using a somatic or physical focus is the most effective way to be present with myself. When I imagine my body from the inside and pay attention to my body feelings, I can see and support energy moving through me more effectively. I can see and feel when my energy gets stuck, like with water, if it stands too long it can become stagnant.

What does stuck energy look like? Some possibilities are: repetitive thought patterns; repetitive symptoms of discomfort in the body such as shaking, nervous habits, lack of circulation, stomach aches or headaches, nausea; chronic muscle or joint pain, allergies, lack of energy or care or curiosity; repetitive behaviors that don't work or resolve something; emotional distance; profound spacing out; the inability to think clearly; attitudes that view life as hard or meaningless.

What does flowing energy look like? Some possibilities are: new and innovative thoughts; a bouncy or energized body feeling; enough energy, care and curiosity to meet new challenges or even old ones; behaviors that adapt to the situation at hand; emotional presence; focus; clear thinking; attitudes that view life as an adventure or a journey.

PRESENCE (n.)

Buddhists call it mindfulness. Scientists call it being observant. Body psychotherapists call it witnessing or awareness. Presence, Awareness, Paying Attention, Witnessing, Observation, Mindfulness. These are all words that mean paying attention to our actions, thoughts, feelings, surroundings and interactions in each moment. Presence is our full awareness of our experience in the moment.

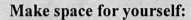

Practice
Being Present

Make space for yourself:

• Using your imagination see your internal space as expandable, or a very large channel or tunnel.

I like to imagine that I am a tunnel under a beautiful bridge in the park. I am a large, echoing chamber with a high ceiling and wide bright openings on either end. I can feel the wind blowing through and the air is bright and moving. Imagining myself as this space gives me a feeling of containment and flow at the same time. There's enough room for me and something much, much bigger than me to move through the space without any problem, like the wind through the tunnel.

Often when we are even mildly stressed out or uncomfortable we contract physically and energetically. We limit the flow of energy.

• **Remove judgment.** Pay attention but try not to analyze or critique your experience or your feelings or your stories in any way. Just notice them. Let everything that's there, just be there - thoughts, feelings, etc. You can even notice if you think this is stupid or you don't have time for such frivolity.

Removing judgement creates psychological space.

Pay attention to your body feelings:

• Notice body feelings. Temperatures, textures, location, depth, energy, contrast, color. You may notice hot, cold, thick, airy, soft, pokey. You will have your own perceptions and words. This makes room for your body.

For example one of my most noticeable feelings is when I feel very hot and very cold at the same time and it feels as if my body has been canceled out and I am completely hollow. Thankfully this doesn't happen very often.

NANA'S BIG
SURPRISE

Body feelings are often attached to emotional feelings. When you pay attention to the body, you are also paying attention to your heart, because it is a part of you. In *Nana's Big Surprise*, you can watch how her feelings move and shift through the imagery of her heart. You can imagine the different ways her body might feel when her heart is in her stomach or in her suitcase or on the swinging folds of her dress when she's dancing.

If you pay attention to body feelings, especially the uncomfortable ones, without judgment, you may begin to notice that emotions can move through more quickly and with greater ease. When this becomes a habit, more and more feelings can move through easier and easier. You are more present which expands your capacity to hold more. Now more energy can freely move through you. This includes creative energy.

The exercise above is to assist you in practicing presence with yourself. You can experiment with this any time during the day. There are no rules to duration. I find that

PRESENCE

I make a point of stopping and being very present when either I, or someone I'm with, is having a lot of uncomfortable feelings. This is when many of us tend to distance or *"try to get away"* from the feelings. Let's look at the boy in the story from the beginning of the chapter for a moment. As he began to create a piece of art that was a reflection of himself, for reasons uniquely his own, he froze. His creative energy was unable to flow and his sense of self was that of defeat and inability. I could see this in his body and hear it in his repetition of words. When I stopped, I paid attention to all of him. His body, his words, his heavy defeated energy as well as his courage, his beauty, his strength and resilience. I knew both defeat and resilience existed in him as it had in me as a child. In paying attention to him, in a sense I was creating an image of him in my imagination, a work of art: a reflection of him. By internally acknowledging all of his experience: defeat and resilience, fear and courage and then saying *"ART IS AN ACT OF COURAGE"* I essentially gave him my image of him, my reflection. This expanded his available perceptions. As John Waterstone, body psychotherapist, suggests I was calling the boy into existence by seeing him and as Scott Jeffrey, theorist, suggests I was changing the situation through observing him. The results speak for themselves.

CREATIVITY

At times, making art can feel hard to students. If you can do the projects yourself first, you will have a similar experience as the children. You would know what parts were hard for you and in what ways. Why could this be useful? Recall from *Chapter 3* that research has shown that most adults have a 4th grade level of creativity. Education theorists believe it's because our culture and schools teach us to not take risks and to adjust ourselves to external expectations that do not support developing more complex ways of thinking. They are finding that this greatly limits our ability to be creative. You may be like many others who find that the idea of doing the art projects feels out of reach. Using presence and *THE 3 RULES*, you have a form to perhaps renegotiate and reclaim some of your own creative energy and belief patterns. Everyone is an artist, including you! You and your students can learn the same lesson, creating *Universal Reflection* between the two of you.

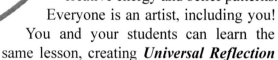

When I have done workshops with educators, most were secretly aching to have an excuse to sit down and make art. None considered themselves artists to begin with. But what they created and the stories they told were complex and beautiful and brave. You can become a direct reflection of the experience your students are having of constantly facing the unknown and doing things for the first time. When something feels hard to do for a student, you can honestly join with them and share something like, *"I know. I got stuck at this point too."*

Beginning with yourself creates an internal pattern, an energetic map of being present with the unknown. How you are BEING broadcasts a clear non-verbal message. It creates an environment around you that makes it easier and more natural for your students to be present. And it will make it more relevant for you to pay attention to them because you will relate to what they are working through with the projects. The child will see you being fully present with yourself first and with them second. This shows them what it looks like and what it feels like to be around presence.

What Does Being Present Do:

- **Supports energy flow**
- **Changes what you observe**
- **Allows you to know yourself more**
- Creates an internal pattern
- Supports yourself to be who you are
- Sets a tone in the classroom
- Let's you teach through being/be a model

BEING PRESENT WITH YOUR STUDENTS

I am not suggesting you teach your students to be present in the way that I am recommending for you to be present with yourself. It's more that if you can hold the basics of presence in thought and practice, it will be easier for them to emulate you. You will be their model.

If we use making art as a tool to know our self, there is the possibility that discomfort and difficult feelings will come up. The CLAIMING FACE curriculum developed as a container for that very thing first for me and then for the children I worked with. We nurture a relationship with creativity as a playground to reflect, express, explore, empower, be free, and expand. Presence is introduced as a backdrop to the curriculum, an understory in a way. Reflection and presence. Clearly they are related. They can work back and forth with each other. Working with our reflection, we are naturally being present with our self. When I stopped and paid attention to the boy and his discomfort in the story, when I was present with him, I created a momentary reflection.

One of the strongest messages we can receive is non-verbal. There is always a moment, however brief, when we can fully stop and pay complete attention to a child. Really look at them. The more we notice, the more we are reflecting back. Inside, notice

COURAGE (n.)

means that you are afraid.
You are aware of your fear. And you make enough room for your fear to exist within you while you do what you know is right for you in the moment.

how they're sitting, how they hold their face, how they hold their pencil or pastel, are they pulled up close to the desk or sitting far away. If you feel stuck then rely on *THE 3 RULES*. They are rooted in years of experience and can help to navigate what arises for children and for adults. They are a built-in support for presence and expansion. Lean on *ART IS ALWAYS AN ACT OF COURAGE*. Right away there is more room to expand into.

When I'm working in the classroom I stop completely with a child. I kneel or lean down until we are eye to eye, even if we don't make eye contact. Often I notice children need to look closely at me, but may not be able to maintain eye contact. This is perfect. We want them to see us being present with ourselves and with them. It is important to stop at some point and be fully present, even for a moment with each child. There may be some children who remind you of yourself, like when I first started going into schools. This is an opportunity for you to simultaneously be present with yourself as you are present with that student. Just notice yourself silently and be curious. You don't need to analyze. Be present and trust that you will know what you need to know about this reminding when you're ready. This makes sure that all of the students are treated equally in terms of respect, being seen, and belonging whether they bring up feelings for you personally or not.

"There is always a moment, however brief, when we can fully stop and pay complete attention to a child."

Sometimes during assemblies, eye contact is all I have. I try to stop and really look at any and all children looking at me. I smile, or give some small sign of awareness just between me and each child. This often elicits their eyes opening even wider and some kind of smile, huge or flicker-y. It's just a small moment of presence, but I've found that children recognize this and remember it. It matters when someone sees us.

PRESENCE

PRESENCE WITH HARD FEELINGS

On occasion someone will ask me, *"what if a student has a lot of feelings come up while making art? What should I do?"* I have had experiences of strong feelings coming up for students. The boy in the story at the beginning of the chapter is just one example that I share because through him, I came to know my *3RD RULE. ART IS ALWAYS AN ACT OF COURAGE.* Feelings do come up. That makes sense and it is ok. I use the word **courage** because real courage does not mean we are not afraid. **We are afraid**. We just find a way to do what we need to do anyway. There is nothing wrong with fear. Usually just making room for something and not resisting it changes the whole experience. This is about expanding presence.

If you have a particularly stressed out student, on rare occasion, body feelings could rise that distract them too much. You could suggest: *"let's stop for a moment and notice."* Say, *"you are making art; this could be courage rising up. Let's pay attention and see how it moves through you."* There may or may not be words for the student. If their body feelings are visible to you, you could say, *"I imagine you might feel hot or cold or fast or heavy. I don't know, but I know you know how you feel. There's nothing wrong with feelings. They're just feelings."* In *Chapter 5*, in *How Do I Let Go and Express My Emotions in My Art*, I discuss how you can use your body to express in moments like these. But most importantly, watch the student. The body feelings might increase in intensity but usually if watched closely, even in silence, they will reach an end point and then slowly come back down. Stay very calm and present with yourself as you witness the student. The two of you can watch the body feelings go up and down. Don't hurry. Trust that they know their way down. You can share your awareness of these things, for example, *"I know that feelings sometimes rise, but they know their way down."*

All this can happen in a matter of minutes. You would be surprised how much can be noticed in a short time when we slow down. Usually we are moving too fast or are far too distracted and externally focused to notice these things. But it is worth paying attention because usually when the energy comes back down the student will feel lighter, even more energized. They may be able to think more clearly and create something even better than they had initially imagined. Through the act of creating the projects, art is used as a container for the experience. Generally, the educator just needs to be solid in their self and hold the philosophies and rules. The importance of reflection, focus on process not product, witnessing, presence, suspension of judgment, *THE 3 RULES*, these are all handy to support the student in allowing the creative force to remain in motion.

Being Present with Your Students:

- Completely stop for a moment with each child

- Try to be at eye level

- Silently notice everything they are experiencing, including their facial expressions and how they hold their body

- You can make eye contact or pay close attention to their art or squeeze their arm

- You can remind them of the 3rd rule

- You can give brief verbal acknowledgment of their physical presence, for example: *I notice that you're not picking up your pencil and you're staring at your desk.*

Remember When You are Present with your Students, You are:

- Giving them an example of someone being present with them

- Naturally changing the dynamic and creating more energy to flow for the student and the classroom

- Expanding the experience which leads to more available possibilities

Presence In The Classroom

Being present with ourselves and with our students sets the tone to bring presence into the classroom. Outlined here are guidelines that have worked for me in providing an overall style that mirrors and perpetuates the philosophies and *THE 3 RULES*. These guidelines keep the focus on process and self awareness while creating the projects.

CHILDREN WITH THEIR OWN ART

When our art looks like us, it is excellent practice to treat and speak well of it. We are using our image as a surrogate to practice treating ourselves respectfully.

How to share and speak about art:

- Students never have to speak about their art/They can always pass

- Keep words focused on the physical attributes of the art, for example materials, colors, shapes

- Speak respectfully about art and the process of learning

Generally, if we feel that we belong and can express freely, we want to share. Sharing can give a feeling of completion and is another way that we give ourselves back to ourselves, in community. However, let sharing develop organically for each student.

EDUCATOR WITH ART

As the educator, practice speaking respectfully about your own art and yourself as an artist in front of the students. This is another opportunity to model.

As with paying attention to yourself, focus on the physical elements of your art. Do this when you show your own art and if you say anything to a student about their art.

For example with a student, instead of saying *"that's so pretty,"* you would say, *"I see that you used oil pastels to color the forehead blue with stars. It reminds me of a night sky. I see that you have completely whited out the eye area and have a flame of red across the throat."*

This image may have many feelings, memories, emotions attached to it for the student. They may or may not be aware of them. As we know some students may have challenging experiences occurring in their life. They may need to express, but there may not be words, or words may not feel appropriate or accessible. Speaking about art in concrete physical terms helps the student and the educator stay present in the most basic sense. The art holds the experience. It is a strong enough container to hold anything. And without specific naming or interpretation, other students who view the art are freer to see themselves reflected there also.

"Speaking about art in concrete physical terms helps the student and the educator stay present in the most basic sense."

REVERENCE/RESPECT

As previously mentioned, by 4th grade many of us have "adjusted" ourselves. We may be inauthentic and hold ourselves to externally prescribed requirements. This can be tricky to renegotiate, especially for adults who may have been doing this for a lifetime. With the CLAIMING FACE curriculum we're using art as a place to practice presence which means being and seeing ourselves for who we really are. This empowers us and leads to self-respect. We want to encourage self-respect as much as possible.

EDUCATOR MODEL OF SELF-RESPECT

An immediate and simple way to begin shifting away from self-judging, over-critical ways of perceiving our self is through verbal language. Encourage yourself to make one small verbal change at a time. A good practice is to speak about the art you create in curious and respectful words. Try not to make excuses or be unkind about what you say about your art. It's good to be learning. It's good to be curious and not know what you're doing. This

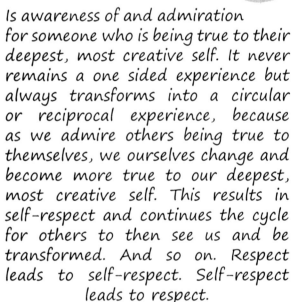

RESPECT (n.)

Is awareness of and admiration for someone who is being true to their deepest, most creative self. It never remains a one sided experience but always transforms into a circular or reciprocal experience, because as we admire others being true to themselves, we ourselves change and become more true to our deepest, most creative self. This results in self-respect and continues the cycle for others to then see us and be transformed. And so on. Respect leads to self-respect. Self-respect leads to respect.

is a great venue to create supportive internal patterns that will build and evolve for yourself as well as serve as a model for your students.

RESPECT YOUR STUDENTS AND TEACH SELF-RESPECT

Extend this same kind of respect to your students, and encourage them to respect themselves. Remind your students to speak about themselves in relation to *THE 3 RULES*, for example *"I AM AN ARTIST."*, *"THERE'S NEVER A RIGHT OR WRONG WAY TO MAKE ART."* And of course, when complicated feelings arise *"ART IS ALWAYS AN ACT OF COURAGE."* We don't dismiss or repress feelings. We give them more space to move through us. This way we can keep the energy flowing so we can do what we need to do. This is an act of respecting ourselves and our experience.

"When we make room for any and all emotion every step along the way of making art, we are making room for ourselves."

RULE THREE IS FOR CREATING ART AND SHARING ART

"ART IS ALWAYS AN ACT OF COURAGE." This is important to remember when making art, *and* when sharing art. When we make room for any and all emotion every step along the way of making art, we are making room for ourselves. Learning to be ourselves all the time, including when we are visible to others, makes us stronger. Over time this practice steadily builds a confidence that is rooted within. This creates a pattern of success and belonging, affecting all aspects of life.

CLASSROOM PRACTICES:

The 3 Rules:

- Classroom environment is rooted in *THE 3 RULES*.

- Display and refer to the *RULES*.

- Encourage everyone to follow the *RULES* together as a class. Ask the students what they think are some good ways for the class to follow the rules.

MORE CLASSROOM PRACTICES:

Art and Sharing:

- We do not touch each other's art. Unless of course, it is a collaborative piece.

- We don't want to single out certain people as *THE ARTIST* in the classroom. We all make art. That is why the projects are not specifically skill-focused, but expression-focused. Everyone is empowered to express.

- Create a specific setting for sharing art. Make a time and a ritual. Everyone has a moment to share about their work if they choose. Others listen.

- When we understand *THE 3 RULES*, we know not only to speak respectfully about other's art, but we allow others to speak about their own art.

For the Educator:

- Projects are never graded. They can be marked as completed.

- Demonstrate how to cut or smear for a project, but only demonstrate the basics. Leave room for students to discover the process on their own.

- It is wonderful for you to share your own projects. But only after your students have completed theirs. Do not use it as an example.

- Share your experience of doing the project. This is your opportunity to be a model, a reflection, and fellow artist.

- Include your art when the class displays a project! This models *Universal Reflection*. You and the students stand together as artists, equal.

For the Children:

- It is a good practice to call each other "artist" when creating or sharing art.

Remind students that *THE 3 RULES* apply to everyone. Use them as a tool to create respect, empathy, and equality. For example, you could say something like, *"Nina looks like she's having a moment of courage. I understand how that feels. Have you ever had to remind yourself of the 3rd rule while making art?"*

Creating Space to Know Self

What truly matters in the CLAIMING FACE curriculum is expanding creative potential and developing a strong sense of self. In the diagram below are some basic supports that provide space around a child. These elements of the curriculum give a child room to relax and grow into themselves on their own terms.

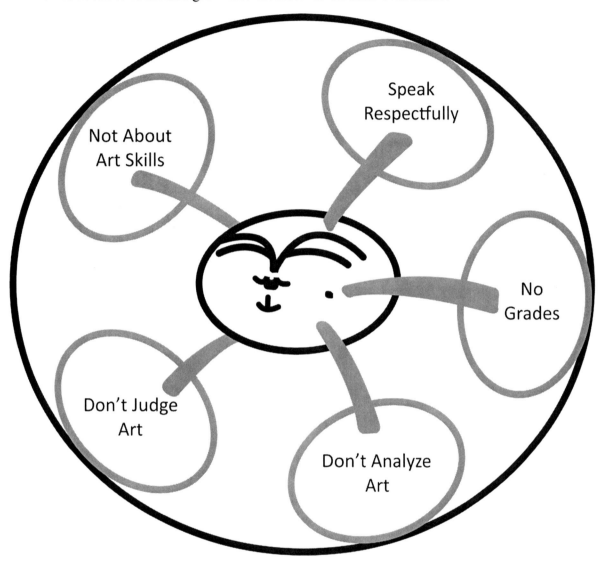

- Because the curriculum is **not about art skills**, materials are kept simple, beautiful and familiar to support success. Realizing that you can create beautiful art is a powerful feeling, especially if it is art about yourself.

- **No grades** removes any structure of right/wrong, good/bad or even the need to perform or disappoint. The art is for the student.

- **Not judging art** makes sure that all creative expression is supported.

- **Not analyzing art** leaves it up to the artist to know what their work means.

- Always, **speak respectfully** about art. Using self-portraiture as the tool to empower makes this very personal work.

Imagine Presence

What is the weather today? Do you like this weather? Does it remind you of anything? What is the color of the sky, the temperature of the air, is it wet or dry? Can you feel the wind? Can you see the wind? Or rain? Or snow? Is this your favorite season?

Can you see nature? Trees? Grass? Birds? Dogs? Do you have a cat? Can you hear a river?

What have you eaten? Did it taste good? Did you have enough time? Are you hungry now? Or full?

How does your body feel? Strong? Weak? Tired? Alert? Achy? Cold? Hot? Just right?

Who have you spoken to today? What did you say? Was this at home? Out in the world? At school?

What are you wearing? What colors, textures, weight? Do you like these colors? Are they comfortable clothes? Are your shoes comfortable? Can you feel your body inside your clothes? Inside your shoes?

Did you go to school today, to work or to learn? Did you drive? Where are you right now? Look around at your environment.

Is your mind open? Or filled with thoughts? If filled, what kind of thoughts? Do you usually think these thoughts? Or are they entirely new thoughts based on the moment?

What are your emotions today? Happy? Sad? Angry? Afraid? Confused? Calm? Distracted? Thoughtful? Happy then distracted? Don't know?

Are there stories in your head right now? About you? Someone in your life? The past? The future?

Just notice everything. No judgment. You are stopping to pay attention to yourself as much as possible. *What else is there?*

Can you sense there is something underneath? Something you can't quite make out, but you know it is there? Notice one last thing about yourself. Something only you would know to notice.

Keep noticing. This is your day. Your life. Your self. Draw anything. Write anything.

Reflect

Keys to Remember from Chapter 4:

What does being *Present* mean

- Being *Present* means that we are aware of ourself as much as possible especially our body.
- Body feelings are often attached to emotional feelings.

What does being *Present* do

- Supports energy flow.
- Changes what you observe.
- Allows you to know yourself more.

Being *Present* with Self

- Make internal space with your imagination.
- Remove judgement.
- Pay attention to your body feelings.
- Refer to the exercise on page 50 to practice presence with yourself. Experiment anytime during the day. There is no set duration.
- Beginning with yourself creates an internal pattern that is easier for your students to emulate.

Being *Present* with Students/Hard Feelings

- Stop fully with each student.
- Pay attention to the students facial expressions and how they hold their body.
- Remind your student of the *3RD RULE, "ART IS ALWAYS AND ACT OF COURAGE."*

Being *Present* in the Classroom and with Art

- Students never have to speak about their art, they can always pass.
- Focus on physical descriptions of art.
- Speak respectfully about self, art, students, and facing the unknown.
- Allow everyone to speak about their own art.
- *EVERYONE IS AN ARTIST.* Don't single anyone out as "The Artist" in the class.
- Create a specific setting to share art.
- Projects are never graded.

Being *Present* with *The 3 Rules*

- Post the *RULES* in the classroom.
- Refer to the *RULES* frequently.
- Engage the students in determining how to follow the *RULES* as a class.

CHAPTER 5

Expression, Standards, and Artistic Development

*P*resence begins small, with oneself in the moment. The more adept we get at it at this level the easier it is to take the next step. We can then let it expand to bring awareness to larger and larger frames of reference. We can see our lives, what is affecting us and affecting our expression more and more clearly. The more we free our expression the more we can know who we are. The more we know ourselves, the more we know our strengths and desires. This empowers us to make choices that fulfill are truest self and live our best life. So it is valuable to allow our presence and awareness to expand to encompass as much of our life and our world as possible. In this chapter I look at some of the larger influences that could be affecting expression. What is important to us? What strengthens us the most to create a good life? What would be the result if everyone understood their distinct individuality and the value of what they have to contribute and to express?

While on the subject of expression, I also explore some ways to express emotions and close with how to support someone who wants to pursue creativity as a fine artist. Truly everyone is an artist, but some of us make a life out of it.

Freeing Expression

Expression is affected by the small and the large elements in our life. From our most intimate settings, such as family, school and religion to our larger cultural contexts, such as our ethnic and social ties, to where we reside, even the era in which we live. It takes focused effort to draw our attention inward away from outside messages, but this brings us closer to our more individual and authentic personal expression. While most of us cannot escape and don't want to escape many of the influences affecting our lives, it is good to bring awareness to them. The larger elements of life are often hard to see. They serve as basic assumptions, so basic that they become invisible. One of these is gender stereotypes. If presenting as a girl or a boy could affect our expression, what else could there be? Curiosity supports creativity and always frees up expression. Be very curious. Be a detective. This can help expose other basic life assumptions that may limit or adjust expression.

GENDER STEREOTYPES/ DECIPHERING THE PRINCESS

Gender stereotypes are one of the most powerful influences in our current culture. Most children know at an early age the clear lines between what kind of expression is acceptable for girls and what is acceptable for boys. We continue to have relatively rigid gender roles. When I go into the schools, it's generally the boys who draw trucks, cars and monsters and the girls who focus on princesses, clothes and flowers. As independent as I've always thought I was, I see the effect of gender stereotypes in my own life. As a child, it is without thought that I drew what was appropriate or expected of me as a girl. I was a princess. For a long time I dismissed it as what girls draw, but I recently deciphered the underlying power of the princess. Not only was I trying to belong and be acceptable like the other girls, but the princess was my available version of a superhero, someone with power.

"The goal is for all children to see themselves for who they really are from their own perspective in their own way."

Gender stereotypes and expectations are very strong. Over the years I've noticed the insideous pressure on girls to express "nice" and "pretty" feelings. Girls are guided to focus on themselves and control and manipulate their personal image to express power. This is demonstrated when girls portray themselves as a "pretty princess" even when heavily challenged in life. Boys are also pressured to express in particular ways although they seem to have a wider range of feelings and experiences that can include anger and even sorrow. Generally boys are allowed to take up more space and be more expressive as long as they're not too nice or too pretty. I've seen boys show themselves with rockets in their bellies and render themselves as torrential rivers. It's important to remember that whether someone is expressing princesses or rockets, the power of their expression is equal.

When I'm making art with children, I make a point of paying the same serious attention to numerous princess and truck drawings as the more explicitly articulate drawings. The more individual drawings often come from the children having the hardest time seeing themselves in what is deemed "acceptable" for their gender. Through the support of the CLAIMING FACE curriculum, all children inevitably grow into more individual and personally expressive imagery. But because of their strong need stressed children are less able to hide or disguise their vulnerability. These children often (literally) illustrate the purpose and power of the curriculum most clearly before less stressed children.

With its strong internal focus, CLAIMING FACE curriculum attempts to free expression from external influences, like gender expectations, that may restrict. The goal is for all children to see themselves for who they really are from their own perspective in their own way.

HOW DO I LET GO AND EXPRESS MY EMOTIONS IN MY ART

"When your drawing originates in your body, you can let your emotion come directly out through your hand."

This is the exact question a boy asked me at an assembly. It was the last question of the day and I was so glad I called on him. It was like having a plant in the audience to ask the most beautiful question possible. I am asked a lot of things, but this was unique. His question seemed loaded with urgency and care.

I told him that one way to begin expressing and letting go into emotion when making art, is to use your body. If you're mad, draw madly. Can you imagine what drawing mad looks like, feels like? How would you hold your pastel mad? Can you feel it all the way up to how you hold your mouth? Now contrast that with a soft, fluffy drawing? Or a flowing drawing? When your drawing originates in your body, you can let your emotion come directly out through your hand. This affects how you create a mark, even how you contact the page. It may not matter what you're drawing. What matters is *how* you're drawing. This is direct, experiential expression. The body is your art tool.

Other times it can be confusing how to express everything in your art, especially deep or complicated feelings or experiences. In *Nana's Big Surprise*, the story is about the grandmother's visit while grieving the loss of the grandfather along with the mishap of the family waiting for eggs from their chickens.

TO EXPRESS (v.)

to allow your internal experience to be manifested externally in some way for you and others to witness.

It's a layered story and I wanted to show both layers: the chicken/rooster surprise as well as the inner story of Nana's heart and her connection to her grandchildren. I used the image of the key for the children, and the heart milagro and shawl for the grandmother. Through this coding the reader can see and explore the familial connections and the inner journey of grief along with the main story through the imagery. (This is described in greater detail in *Behind the Story* in *Chapter 8*.)

NANA'S BIG SURPRISE

In *My Colors, My World* there is also a story inside the story, but it is more coded into the imagery than in *Nana's Big Surprise*. This story opens with a familiar, mundane event. A powerful, blind wind has covered everything with sand, making everything the same color. The wind and sand storm symbolize an overwhelming experience. Often when we experience something very difficult, it can feel like everything in our world goes flat, loses meaning or becomes colorless. This is both a story about a little girl discovering color, but also about finding a sense of self through reflection and the return of curiosity and meaning in her surroundings through searching out color.

MY COLORS, MY WORLD

Projects like *Emotions of Color, What No One Can See* and *Courage Portrait* specifically provide opportunities to explore expressing emotions through art.

Some Ways To Express Emotion in Your Art:

- Use your body to hold the emotion so that how you mark the page is expressive

- Use a symbol to represent an emotion

- Use a symbolic action to represent an experience

Standards, Competence, Confidence and Peace

I am told that student performance standards and testing are a constant and increasing stress for educators. I appreciate the intent that all our children should know reading, writing and arithmetic. I also know that the promise of college is often a drive toward improving economic survival. It is important for all people to feel that they can dream all the dreams and that no matter what their dream is, it is possible to achieve. Everyone deserves equal opportunity as well as social and economic equality.

I understand the importance in part because college was not something that was ever talked about in my home. My father was a lineman and my mother was a homemaker. College was outside of our life. Miraculously, I did end up attending college, but on campus I continued to struggle with an even greater lack of reflection. So when I lost my funding short of finishing two degrees, I just walked away. That's it I figured. Now I have to find my own way.

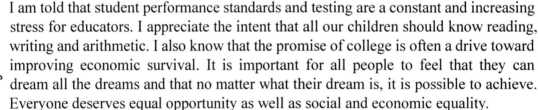

TO SELF-EMPOWER (v.)

Deriving the strength to do something through one's own thoughts and based on the belief that one knows what is best for oneself.

While I would NEVER discourage a child from dreaming and ultimately going to college, I think there is greater meaning in supporting all children in knowing themselves and prioritizing self-empowerment and a strong sense of self. This could lead to college, but not everyone will go to college for many different reasons. There is meaning and importance in **all** work especially if we have a strong sense of self and know our creative potential. Everyone is an artist and everything is **art**. Many will work jobs that only require the most basic skills. Whether a child is college bound or not, I want them to feel competent and confident. Besides the most basic skills, this is the most important thing. We need everyone on every level to make life work. We need machinists like my brother, as much as we need doctors as much as we need bus drivers, as much as we need teachers and artists. I want everyone to have a sense of belonging and know that whether they have a college degree or not, whether they make a certain amount of money or not, their self, their life, all that they contribute is worthwhile and creative. Our current culture is distinctly focused on monetary and generally not emotional reward in relation to life and work. But I am curious if there is a way to support all children for their human potential first and foremost and let their educational, economic and social potential take a step back. I trust that with a strong sense of self, everyone will find their most empowered place and their perfect way to it.

"I trust that with a strong sense of self, everyone will find their most empowered place and their perfect way to it."

I tell students that I study and research and learn and practice all the time. I let them know that sometimes you do not need a degree to do what you love, like being an artist or author. You just need to know that you can do anything. I hope that the philosophy and the experiences related to the CLAIMING FACE curriculum can create a model of equality and respect, as well as enhance deep, creative thinking and a strong sense of self that trusts anything is possible!

Artistic Development

CLAIMING FACE philosophy and curriculum is meant for everyone. Our first rule is that *"EVERYONE IS AN ARTIST."* However, there will be those of us, like me, who are truly hooked by art. But even I cannot say that I would absolutely, definitely have become a fine artist, if I had been exposed to this kind of thinking and work as a child. I cannot know if I had been truly empowered as a young girl, if I would have needed art as much as I have to negotiate invisibility, stress, self-esteem and personal power. I love many, many ways of expressing myself and given a stronger sense of self at a very young age that developed and deepened as I got older, I may have had greater freedom and confidence to choose any number of paths. So while we may have students who will choose art as a serious interest or even a career or vocation, it is important to support everyone equally in becoming all that they are as artists.

I Don't Care if a Chair

I use art as a tool, an excuse to play, to engage and empower. I honestly don't care if a child or an adult for that matter can draw a chair to look like a chair. I adore stick figures and lumpy approximations! What I care about is the process of self-discovery, having a strong sense of self, and belonging. To be honest, art skills can and are more likely to develop this way, but the goal of the CLAIMING FACE curriculum is to **build the powerful link between creativity and a sense of self**. The curriculum projects are kept simple and are specifically geared toward beauty, success, and expression, and specifically <u>not</u> art skills. This curriculum encourages life or self skills using art as a container for the experience. This way all skills that are unique and highly individual have greater freedom to develop. They may not fit prescribed concepts about what one should be "learning about art" which is fine. The confidence to explore as well as know and empower self, is what's important for the students. Students will find their own true way of expression and knowing which will serve them in life more than knowing how to draw an accurate perspective or realistic portrait. **Self and life are the process and ever-evolving product of this focus on creativity.**

"The confidence to explore as well as know and empower self, is what's important for the students."

With that said, I believe the CLAIMING FACE philosophy and curriculum are an excellent backdrop for learning art skills if desired.

When Someone Loves Art

We acknowledge there are many ways to be an artist. We are all artists, but some of us will become more fixated on not only the process, but also the product. We want to remain steady in avoiding any students pointing and proclaiming, *"I'm not an artist. She's the artist!"* in the classroom, because **everyone is engaging in art.** If someone is especially talented or interested in art, do not separate them out as special or fundamentally different. This is just that student's thing. Art is their art, but everyone is an artist. Everyone has an art all their own and has something uniquely individual to express. *The 3 Rules* are there to remind us.

If a student is interested in art beyond what you are covering in the classroom, by all means, point them in a direction that will encourage their exploration. In the

CLAIMING FACE curriculum we're focusing on creativity as a process to know ourselves. This easily accommodates knowing self as a fine artist.

Support your student in such a way that they can continue to discover themselves through the process. Send them to the library to look at art books of all kinds or look for the perfect role model to inspire them. There are also public programs and events at libraries and museums or recreation centers for young fine artists. Provide as much information as possible and they will naturally be drawn to what interests them. There is never a right or wrong way to become a fine artist. **We need all the art we can get in this world!**

Additional Support for a Student Interested in Art

Encourage the student to make a notebook (three ring or a sketch book would work) to hold collected images, such as:

- copies of art from books that inspire them,

- places they need to go to see art or make art,

- artists that they hear about and want to research,

- artists they've met at the library or school events,

- ideas about what to make,

- a place for notes about what they learn about materials, etc…

- everything related to creativity.

They can tape the collected imagery onto pages, have plastic sleeves to put images into and/or punch holes into full sheets to create new pages.

Encourage them to write notes to themselves around, on, or near the collected imagery. In this way they can create an ongoing conversation with their self.

I have many of these kinds of books. I even collect imagery I find out in the world like postcards, flyers, calendars, and more. I make copies of absolutely everything I love on the internet or from magazine pages. I have lists of artists I want to research, and more and more and more and more. I like to get my books out sometimes and just look at everything and see if any art comes of it.

Imagine

Expression

For a moment, put your hand over your mouth. Press tightly. Imagine that you cannot move your hand. Be still. Be very still.

Now become aware of the energy in your body. Remember the circle you drew from Chapter 3. Remember the energy that moves through you. *Can you feel it moving? Can you feel it moving even underneath your hand pressed tightly over your mouth? Can you feel it even through your stillness?*

What do you want to express, but you sense that you are not allowed? What is forbidden? Not appropriate? Beyond the scope of your life, your ability or your right?

What do you want to express, but you don't know how? Can you sense a feeling, a thought, an experience, some way of being? But no matter how you try you cannot form thoughts or words that adequately convey it.

Is there something inside of you that you can see, but it is far, far away? It is on the horizon like a horse frozen in its tracks, unable to move, but filled with energy and a need to run.

When you were a child what were you told about expression? One side of my family said, *"children are seen, but not heard."* The other side liked to say *"I'll give you something to cry about."* Sometimes people tell children to *"be good, don't talk back, behave yourself, girls don't do that, be a man, mind your p's and q's. You're too young for that. Stop crying. Do I have to do everything? Be quiet."*

Feel the energy in your body. Now take your hand off of your mouth. Raise both of your hands and push out. Feel the energy in your body expand up and your energy fill the space around you as far as your stretched out hands. Sense this large space all around you. This is part of your space. Imagine that this space that you have created is completely private. It is even sound proof space and it is all yours. Within this you can say anything, do anything, create anything. Only you will know. **There is no limit.** Here in this space, or any of the other available spaces left open for drawing in the book, scribble a drawing of the first thing you would do or create or say.

Draw it! Claim it!

Reflect

1 When you were a child, what was considered a good child? Was a good girl different than a good boy? Were you considered good? Or bad? Did anyone ever tell you that you had an attitude problem? That you were too emotional or difficult? Did anyone ever tell you to be free? To express everything inside of you exactly the way you wanted, as long as you didn't hurt anything or anyone?

2 What sort of things were you told by parents, teachers and adults in your life about how you should behave? Did you adjust your behavior to accommodate these messages? Were you successful if you did?

3 If you adjusted yourself, how did it feel? Were you rewarded in any way?

4 Were there specific expectations of you in your family, at school, with your friends, in the world? Did these expectations match your internal feelings? Did they match the dreams you had for yourself when you grew up?

5 What do you think affected you the most growing up?

KEYS TO REMEMBER FROM CHAPTER 5:

- Many outside influences affect our creative expression: family, school, religion, ethnic and social ties, gender, the era we live in.

- Be curious to see what could be affecting expression.

- Girls are expected to express "pretty" and "nice" things. Boys are expected to take up more space and express more, as long as it is not too nice or pretty.

- Pay attention to princesses and trucks as much as more individual and articulate imagery.

- Stressed out children demonstrate the power of the curriculum first.

- Ways to let go and express emotion in art:
    - use your body to hold the emotion.
    - use a symbol to represent experience or emotion.

- Support all children for their **human potential** first and foremost.

- Life skills supersede art skills.

- Art skills are more likely to develop but are not a focus with this curriculum.

- Resources for students who want to pursue fine art:
    - go to the library to research art, artists and role models.
    - go to public art programs in libraries, museums and recreation centers.
    - make an artist's notebook.

CHAPTER 6

The 3 Rules

And finally, ***THE 3 RULES***! The basics of the philosophies and knowings of the CLAIMING FACE curriculum are distilled into ***THE 3 RULES***. This makes it easy to carry the information into the classroom. Calling them rules makes us stop and pay attention. However, I see them more as universal truths. My job is to notice these truths and bring attention to them. I encourage you to play with the rules relentlessly.

THE 3 RULES should be:

- Discussed and explored for greater understanding
- Visibly posted
- Frequently repeated to glean full support
- Encouraged in every way to be personally claimed by each child and educator

THE 3 RULES developed alongside the curriculum to hold the artist through the process and experience of the projects. The rules are characterized by two experiences that result from using them with the projects. For example, ***EVERYONE IS AN ARTIST*** provides us with a new reflection as an artist and a new purpose to EXPRESS through art! For easy navigation the projects are categorized by these experiences. This helps contextualize each project's purpose and meaning. Each rule also includes a "theory" to help you better explain them to your students.

THE 3 RULES do not stand alone. They support and layer one upon the other. They interact and weave together to create a strong support. As the rules are described in greater detail, watch how even the words defining each individual rule weave back and forth across the other rules.

Rule #1: Everyone is an Artist.

Experiences:

Reflection
this rule creates a new reflection, it reframes us as artist.

Express
with our new expanded reflection we have a new purpose, an artist's job is to express.

Further supported by: The ***Polka Dot*** Theory

Rule #2: There is never a right or wrong way to make art.

Experiences:

Explore
this rule removes pressure so we are free to explore and express without fear.

Empower
without external judgement, we are the authority of who we are and what we express.

Further supported by: The ***Boss of Me*** Theory

Rule #3: Art is always an act of courage.

Experiences:

Freedom
this rule creates space to accept any and all of our feelings.

Expand
when we do not press our feelings down, we have more space and can expand.

Further supported by: ***Mistakes are Moments of Courage*** Theory

Rule #1: Everyone is an artist.

Reflection / Express

Reflection. This rule creates a new reflection. It reframes us as artist. This rule gives permission to grow into this larger perception of self as creative.

Express. Within our new, expanded reflection we have a new purpose. An artist's job is to express. The rule comes full circle in the CLAIMING FACE curriculum, because our **new reflection** as an artist is to express and create our **own reflection**.

RULE #1 is a unifying and **empower**ing statement. It immediately creates a tone of equality and inclusion among everyone, out of which arises respect and curiosity. It confirms that everyone has something valuable to contribute and inspires a sense of wonder about what that might be for each of us. It acknowledges the force of creativity that flows through all of us and through that acknowledgement we become larger. We can each say: I am artist; I create; I contribute; I am. This first rule begins the powerful link between creativity and a sense of self.

POLKA DOT THEORY

I have witnessed much art making in my work and I have noticed that no one marks the page the same way. Literally, our very bodies carry our uniqueness. If I make a polka dot on the page and you make one and another person makes one, we can tell who made which polka dot. How we carry our stories and experiences affects how we hold our hand, touch a pencil, apply pressure and execute something as basic as a dot. Just a dot expresses something that is all our own. My polka dot is mine and only mine. And yours can only be yours. This is the beginning of art and being an artist.

Rule #2: There is never a right or wrong way to make art.

Explore / Empower

Explore. When we realize that there is not a right or wrong way to be ourselves and express what we must, a pressure is taken off. We are freed to explore and express without fear of wrong doing or living up to what is "right."

Empower. All art is self-portrait. No one can express what is ours to express better than ourselves. In this way we can know ourselves and express ourselves for who we really are. We are literally our own authority of who we are and what we express.

RULE #2 is a **free**ing statement. It takes judgment off of creativity and frees up the relationship with the self so the artist can create authentically.

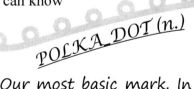

POLKA DOT (n.)

Our most basic mark. In this simple mark we see our unique self in how we hold our stories in our hand, how we hold a pencil, contact the page, and create.

 75

Through this the artist can learn from and know themselves. By extension it supports an open stance for others to create as they see fit. Without judgment, our creative possibilities, and even our possibilities of who we are and can become, **expand**.

I AM THE BOSS OF ME

If something as simple as a polka dot can show something that is uniquely our own, imagine what doing more than a polka dot can do. Everything we create shows something about ourselves. Ultimately, who else can be the "expert," the "boss of you," but you! No one can know you more than you. No one can BE more you, then you! So how can you be you or show you in the "wrong" way? It's not possible!

Rule #3: Art is always an act of courage.

Freedom / Expand

Freedom. This rule creates space for us to accept any and all of our feelings. I use courage to begin with because this includes fear. This is a doorway to all layered and complex feelings. The point is that we are free to feel what we feel. This rule echoes the 2nd rule in that it frees us from judgment, but this time in relation to emotional expression instead of creative expression.

Expand. When we do not press our feelings down, but instead provide room and acknowledgment of our feelings, they can move around and through. This creates more internal space and increases our capacity to deal with our emotions and allow energy to flow. The more space we have, the more we can expand.

RULE #3 is an acceptance statement. As we engage with creativity, the nonverbal, the unknown or unexpressed inside of us seeks **express**ion. This may be all the more necessary if we are not accustomed to seeing ourselves reflected in our world. There are bound to be feelings that move through us. These may come in the form of thoughts, emotions or body feelings. When we honestly and authentically come face to face with ourselves and all we have experienced in our lives at this time, this is an act of courage. For us to then let that become the physical document of art, when we create a **reflection** of who we really are, it is even more courageous. We are claiming ourselves. Courage doesn't mean we're not afraid. There may be fear. We just find a way to do what we need to do while we are afraid. There's nothing wrong with fear.

MISTAKES ARE MOMENTS OF COURAGE

Although I've made hundreds of paintings, I still sometimes face the blank page and think; *I don't know what I'm doing! How do I do this? Why do I do this? This is hard.* I begin drawing, but feel unsure. Every line feels like a mistake. I want to crumple up my piece of paper and start over again. But what I've found to be true is not that I've necessarily made a mistake, but that this is a moment of courage. Often, if I just let the "mistake" be there and keep working, things turn around. I often find something wonderful and unexpected in the mistake that I like even more than what I had imagined initially. Not framing things as mistakes, but as moments of courage keeps me curious and open as to what could happen next. I've learned to flow with anything that at first *seems* like a mistake to me. If we know that courage is part and parcel of the creative process and can honor, invite, even use it as a tool to strengthen ourselves, then we are truly artists! Art is not about the product, but about the process. For most of us the art product will fade or shift in importance or meaning with age and time. What lasts, what we cannot discard, is what happens inside of us as we create. That is ours.

Exploring The 3 Rules symbol

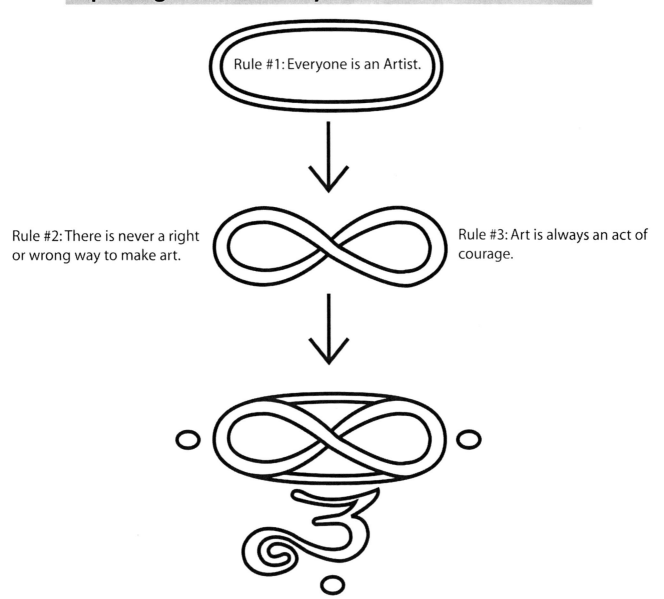

Rule #1: Everyone is an Artist.

Rule #2: There is never a right or wrong way to make art.

Rule #3: Art is always an act of courage.

The oval is the first rule - *EVERYONE IS AN ARTIST*. This rule reframes and contains us as creative. The infinity symbol within the oval represents the second and third rule - *THERE IS NEVER A RIGHT OR A WRONG WAY TO MAKE ART* and *ART IS ALWAYS AN ACT OF COURAGE.* As we engage with creativity we inevitably hit emotional and creative blocks. By constantly reminding ourselves of these two rules we learn to remove judgment from creative and emotional expression. This allows us to maintain an authentic and empowered stance as an artist and keep creative energy flowing.

Imagine Expression

Breathe in, as you breathe out imagine that you are drawing an oval on the ground around you. You are standing perfectly in the center of this oval. Breathe in and feel your energy expand to fill this space, all the way to the very edge of the oval. The entire oval is you. Here, within this oval *you are an artist.*

In your imagination, standing at the center of your oval, you can feel a good sized, round river stone in each of your hands. You can feel the weight of each stone as you bounce one hand up and down and then the other. They are not too heavy, but they are heavy enough. *Does their weight feel equal? Is one a bit heavier than the other?* Bounce one hand then the other, back and forth and in your imagination, feel the weight of each stone.

Look down at the stone in your left hand. You can see that there are words carved beautifully into the texture of the stone. It reads *"there is never a right or wrong way to make art."*

Look down at the stone in your right hand. Again, you see that there are words carved beautifully into the texture of the stone. This one reads *"art is always an act of courage."*

Close your eyes, again feel the weight of these stones in your hands, back and forth. Then remember the oval in which you stand. Feel your feet on the ground. Your own weight holding you in this perfect spot, centered in your oval. You open your eyes again and look at your hands, the stones are gone, but you can still feel their weight. Slowly their weight moves up your arms. It is as if the weight of the stones has been transformed into energy. This energy perfectly matches your own and it moves through your hands and up your arms. As it moves up and into your arms, you feel stronger and stronger. The energy goes to the center of your body and strengthens every part of you.

Open your eyes and draw an oval. Within that oval draw the two stones. As the energy from the stones rose up into your arms it joined the natural flow of the energy in your body. Draw the energy in your body flowing around the two stones you drew in the oval. *You are an artist. There is never a right or wrong way for you to make art. Your art is always an act of courage.*

Reflect

1 What comes to mind when you think of "artist?" How does an artist dress? What concerns an artist? Do artists make decisions and choices differently than those who do not see that they are artists?

2 When you think of yourself as an artist, do you see yourself differently or the same as when you consider yourself a student, a teacher, a parent, a son or daughter, a partner?

3 When you got dressed this morning, brushed your teeth, prepared for the day, did you do it the "right way?" Or did you do it exactly the way you do it? What about now? Are you reading this the "right way" or is the information and your own knowing in relation to it developing in exactly your way?

4 What is the hardest thing you've ever done in your life? How did it feel? What did you learn about yourself? What did you learn about life?

5 Now that the rules have entered your imagination go back to the beginning of Part One to further investigate what they mean to you. They are not only distillations of the philosophy to carry into the classroom for your students. They are yours. How do they serve you? What do you have to teach that is uniquely your own about the rules?

KEYS TO REMEMBER FROM CHAPTER 6:

- ***RULE #1: EVERYONE IS AN ARTIST:***
    - Reflection: self as creative.
    - Express: expanded reflection gives new purpose as artist to express.

- Polka Dot Theory: even a polka dot shows something about ourselves.

- ***RULE #2: THERE IS NEVER A RIGHT OR WRONG WAY TO MAKE ART:***
    - Explore: we are free to explore without the pressure of judgement.
    - Empower: we become our own authority.

- Boss of Me: only we can know, be, and express ourselves.

- ***RULE #3: ART IS ALWAYS AN ACT OF COURAGE.***
    - Freedom: free to have all feelings.
    - Expand: more space for our feelings to move and expand.

- Mistakes and courage are a part of art: not framing things as mistakes but as moments of courage supports students to be curious and open to what could happen next.

PART 2

OUTSIDE

When we have gathered
our thoughts,
our hearts and
our experiences,
what we need are tools.

We travel OUTSIDE to
put the tools in our
hands.

Through an exploration
of the art materials
and the books that
support the projects,
we draw our attention
outward and
prepare ourselves
for action.

Open your hands.

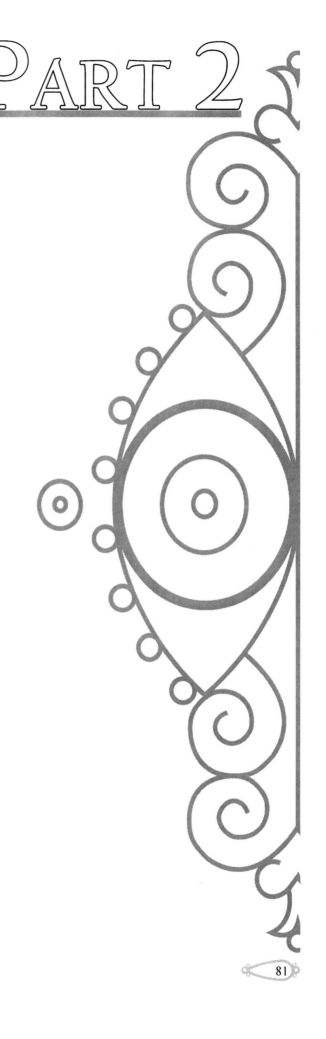

Draw it! Claim it!

Draw it! Claim it!

Draw it! Claim it!

"I am not afraid of your art. Do whatever you need to do."

Materials, Display, & Storage

C uriosity and presence continue into all aspects of creativity, all the way through knowing your materials to storing all the fantastic art that gets made. This is the brass tacks chapter about the physicality of making art. What to use, how to use it, where to use it, and how to show and store what you have made. But as we know, there is a lot to pay attention to when using the CLAIMING FACE curriculum. It's not just about pulling out the paints and calling it a day. Getting familiar with how to let creative energy flow through us also affects the physical aspect of making art. When I am working on a children's book, I expect that my studio will become a mess. I start off organized and create systems to deal with each step of the process. Some hold, some do not. I always have to do a huge cleaning up after every book because during the process, I'm in a whirl and I cannot be bothered with neat little systems. Even if I created them to help myself. Still, I strongly recommend making your creative environment as familiar, organized, and systematic as possible. This creates a container to hold the art experience allowing the creative energy to flow freely and the art to get made without spending the majority of time struggling with organization.

The *Using the Materials* section is designed to be an easy reference for different kinds of materials, how to use them, and my related books. There is also a supply list for a basic student kit and an accompanying classroom kit. Working with photos of the students is a distinctive and necessary tool to the CLAIMING FACE curriculum. In *Working with Photographs* the basics for success are covered. The *Display* and *Storage* sections discuss the importance of showing and storing work respectfully. I cover the overall experience of creating art: set up, organizing materials, storage, display, clean up. Every step counts. Involve students in every area.

Using the Materials

What better time could there be in life than childhood to use the same art materials as fine artists? Childhood is naturally one of the most spontaneous and creative times in our lives. By all means, use the richest colors and the creamiest textures. Draw madly and get dirty. Please!

REAL ART MATERIALS

ART MATERIALS

I think it's fantastic for children to work with "real" art materials whenever possible. While I love a good crayon, I think it's important to demystify "art" and its materials. Art is not something locked away in museums or galleries. And artists are not far away, magically endowed beings. Bringing into the classroom the same kind of materials that artists use and are on display in museums and galleries, like oil pastels and charcoal, makes these tools familiar and accessible. This empowers children to know that they can use them. It also gives a sense of importance and power to the work they create with them. And as great as all this is, using "real" art materials also provides greater depth and variety in visual expression than the materials traditionally provided for children. If there is ever a time to engage with real art materials, it is during the most creative stage of our lives. Toys, even books are often quickly forgotten, but art materials are used up.

COLOR

In most color media like crayons, pastels, and paints, I like to layer colors on top of each other to create greater depth and richness. Even with crayons, I like to layer blues with greens or yellows with greens, reds with pinks or reds with purples. Encourage experimenting with what colors look good layered together or next to each other. Exploring the materials includes how to use them in every conceivable way, as well as, how much color variety you can push out of your materials. If you look closely enough at nearly anything, you can see more color than you initially assumed was present. For example, an apple has red, orange, brown, gold, burgundy...

STANDARDS

CLAIMING FACE curriculum is not focused on art skills. These are more likely to occur, but only in service to personal awareness and expression. We are concerned with process over product. I have consistently found that with this focus children create beautiful and more art because it has personal meaning to them. This generally makes them more open to understanding the requirements of art standards if or when they need to be addressed.

BREAKAGE AND GETTING DIRTY!

Often children want their pastels or crayons or such to be in "perfect" condition. I tell them that one, artists will use anything to make art! And two, I often break my pastels on purpose so that they're easier for me to hold. One of my favorite sayings is, "*if you're getting dirty, you know you're making art!*"

ABOUT THE MATERIALS (ALPHABETICALLY LISTED)

The materials listed over the next pages are generally familiar and easily accessible. I love the old basics like pencils and crayons and they are very good to start with. But gradually use charcoal instead of pencil, oil pastels instead of crayons. Building on familiarity encourages both confidence and exploration. And, using richer materials makes a huge difference in quality and expression. Using a wide range of materials will bring more beauty to the work, adding to the students' experience of it, as well as the visual beauty of your classroom.

ART MATERIALS

As you'll notice, each material lists different styles or types to give ideas of the variety that is available to you. I often elaborate and discuss several of the different types of a material, particularly the ones you may often engage with in the projects, but I do not always go into all of the types listed. This section is meant to be an overview of the materials. Whole books are written about many of these materials, including techniques, tips, and more. So, while I offer a crash course based on my years of experience using these materials, if you want more in-depth discussion about any material check the *Resources* in the back, visit your local library, or search the internet to find out more.

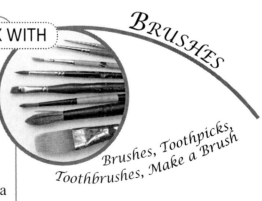

HOW TO WORK WITH

BRUSHES

Brushes, Toothpicks, Toothbrushes, Make a Brush

Use **Soft brushes** for watercolors and inks and **Stiffer brushes** for heavier paints like tempera or for chalk on the sidewalk. When I paint I like to use soft brushes. **Toothbrushes** are fun for splattering paint. **Toothpicks** can be used as tiny ink or paint pens. You could do a watercolor and then when it's dried go back into it using a toothpick as a drawing tool dipped in ink or paint.

Make a Brush: Use any stick, one found outside, a pencil, a chopstick, a craft stick, or a shish kabob stick.
Using thread or wire or tape, or possibly a clever combo of all three, secure hair, thread, yarn or grass to the end of the stick to use as a brush.

CHALK PASTELS

All kinds are Gorgeous!

HOW TO WORK WITH **Chalk pastels** are not soft. They are firm, more like the kind we use on the chalkboard but are a bit crumbly. Use over images or photos or layer and blend with fingers or a chamois cloth (available at art stores). Chalk pastel art should be preserved in a portfolio with another sheet of paper placed over the art or even plastic before storing. Plastic wrap would work. I purchase thick plastic sheeting from a fabric store and cut pieces to fully wrap the piece. There are also plastic sleeves you can purchase at art stores.

CHARCOAL

Vine, Stick, Pencil, White

HOW TO WORK WITH I loved **charcoal** as soon as I met them. Your hands get dirty and for some reason a smudge always gets on the tip of my nose. Covering up desks or clothes can cut down on clean-up when using this material. Charcoal is great for experimenting and it always looks beautiful. Artists have used charcoal for centuries, perhaps it is "the original" art material. It is easy to use. Draw light. Draw hard. Draw with line or shade in blocks and forms. Smudge it with your fingers or with a soft chamois cloth (available at art stores). Fill in an area and use an eraser to mark out texture, light, or pattern. This is sort of the opposite of drawing. As with pastel art, charcoal art should be stored with another sheet of paper or plastic over it to protect the art.

Vine charcoal are thin, bare sticks of charcoal. They are fragile, easily break, and mark more subtly than stick charcoal. I often use vine charcoal to do the first part of a drawing before switching to stick charcoal. I also use it for subtle shading like in *I Know the River Loves Me*.

Stick charcoal is like heaven to me. You can go back and forth between drawing lightly or drawing hard, creating a deep black velvet.

Pencil charcoal has the great attribute of being a pencil, something we are all used to working with. It has a finer line with the attributes of charcoal.

White charcoal challenges us to see in terms of light. This can be mixed in while using black or brown charcoal or it can be used on black or colored paper gorgeously.

BOOKS *I Know the River Loves Me:* I had to be very careful to keep my paper white. I used my eraser a lot and every kind of charcoal listed.

I use a strong **cloth** without any stretch to it. Oil pastels work beautifully on this material. The *I Am Here Flags/Hand Portraits* use oil pastels on cloth. Since cloth is not stiff, tape it down before working on it. Using masking tape, tape down the entire edge of each side of the cloth on a desk or an art board. Masking tape is usually the least expensive and easiest to get on and off the cloth.

Plain, black cotton cloth is easily found at fabric stores. A poly/cotton blend will also work.

HOW TO WORK WITH

CLOTH

Black, Color, Patterned, Cotton, Tight Weave

I gather any liquid proof **containers** that come into my kitchen. **Baby food jars** are my absolute favorite because they are small and have good lids which makes them work for mixing small amounts of color or for water when painting on the go. **Jars, plastic containers** and **cans without lids** work if you clean up after a project or have a space where you can keep things set up. I often have two containers for water because I like my water clean. With two I don't have to get fresh water as often. Flat items, like **meat trays** and **lids**, I use like a palette to mix paints or glue.

HOW TO WORK WITH

CONTAINERS
MIXING & WATER

Cans, Yogurt Cups, Milk and Meat Cartons, Plastic Lids, Containers with Numerous Small Cups, Jars

With **crayons**, I try to push to get as much color and density as possible. I color thick or layer on multiple colors. When I layer, I gather all of one color like all the reds or all the blues and color them on top of each other to create texture, depth, and richer, more complex colors. One day I hope to do a book in crayons as I think they are a fabulous art material.

HOW TO WORK WITH

CRAYONS

Have As Many Colors As Possible!

I love my trusty **pencil end eraser**, but for large areas I use a **hand held eraser** and for tight spots and more delicate paper I use a **kneaded eraser**. It's fun to use erasers on large penciled in areas. Blend, create texture, shading, or pattern. I usually use erasers when I draw, but not always.

I Know the River Loves Me: I used charcoal to create the little girl. If you look closely you can see that I used a kneaded eraser to blend and shade. It gives it a soft, smooth look.

HOW TO WORK WITH

ERASERS

Pencil End, Handheld, Kneaded

BOOKS

GLUE & GLITTER GLUE

White, Glue Stick, Modge Podge, Paste

HOW TO WORK WITH I have had to learn a lot about **glue** for many of my books. I have made collages out of cut photos, copies on cardstock, and all kinds of paper. I generally use modge podge and paste to make the collages.

White Glue is good for gluing small items like buttons or foil, but not as good for paper.

Use **Glitter Glue** as a wonderful accent on paintings and drawings of all kinds as a final touch. Use glitter glue for gluing 3D objects to add a little sparkle.

A **Glue Stick,** I think, is the best for most paper projects. It's not messy and holds well.

Use **Modge Podge** and **Paste** for serious collaging. Modge Podge is comparable to white glue, but leaves a nicer finish and can be diluted with water. I use paste for the initial paste down because it remains flexible.

BOOKS *Animal Poems of the Iguazu*: I used many different papers to create the background. I cut and glued every piece.

Nana's Big Surprise: I glued cut photos onto my paintings to create clothes and the chicken coop.

Angels Ride Bikes and Other Summer Poems: I printed photos in black & white on cardstock and glued them down into the drawings and then painted over them.

INK

Bottle or Cake

HOW TO WORK WITH **Inks** are tricky to work with but oh so fun. It's less like painting and more like drawing. The inks are smooth and flow easily, be loose and free. The ink comes in small bottles so set up a stable space as inks love to get knocked over. I sometimes set my ink bottles in a small box to keep them stable. Ink cakes are an alternative. Find these either at an art store or a Japanese stationary store. Small "calligraphy kits" are available that include the ink cake or stick, a brush, a mixing block and a brush stand. Like oil paints, these may be a bit difficult for the classroom, but are good to know a little about especially when looking at the amazing art of Asian calligraphy. They usually come with a small instruction booklet that explains how to set up the ink with water on the ink block.

BOOKS *I Know the River Loves Me:* I used ink to "draw" my friends, the river and woods.

Ring binders are easy to get from the store, but almost anything can be made into a **journal**. Use a heavier paper like cardstock to make the cover and then fill with any paper you can find. You can even use recycled paper that is printed on the back. To secure a binding, use a hole punch and brads, staples, a sewing machine, or hand sewing. Or, glue all the pages together on the binding side and then glue a strip along the spine to finish the cover. Use paper, tissue, or cloth for the spinal strip.

HOW TO WORK WITH

JOURNAL

Handmade, Ring Binder

BOOKS

My Diary From Here to There:
Journals can be for art as well as words.

Permanent Markers are a favorite when I play with young children. They are vibrant and easy to work with and can even be used on foil. Markers mix well with other materials like watercolors and crayons. They are permanent though, so cover clothes and work areas if that's a problem. **Thick tip markers** work for filling in or creating bold outlines, while **thin tips** make fine, detailed patterns.

HOW TO WORK WITH

MARKERS

Permanent Markers, Fine Tip, Thick Tip

Oil Pastels are beautiful on colored paper, especially black, as well as cloth and plain paper. Because they are soft you can smear them, layer them or blend them together with great ease. Carve into them with pencil tips, fingernails, or pennies on your art. Layer over watercolors or try watercolors on top of them. They are dramatic over images, like in the *Frida Mirror* and *Photo Self-Portrait* projects.

HOW TO WORK WITH

OIL PASTELS

Even The Cheapest Brands are Gorgeous!

Oil Pastels can be messy because of their softness. Having something covering the desk or even clothes cuts down on clean up. This also means that storage is more of a delicate job. Preserve oil pastel art in a portfolio and place another sheet of paper or plastic over the art before storing. Plastic wrap would work. I purchase thick plastic sheeting from a fabric store and cut pieces to fully wrap the piece. There are plastic sleeves of all kinds available at art stores for preservation and storage.

My Very Own Room: Look closely at this book. You can see the actual markings of the oil pastels, as well as the blending and layering.

BOOKS

OPTIONAL OBJECTS

Buttons, String, Yarn, Foil, Found Objects: "trash," recyclables, plant matter, wood, photos, cards, junk mail, magazines

HOW TO WORK WITH

Objects add a fascinating dimension to your work. White glue and glitter glue love 3D objects. You can use found objects that you collect or gather in your environment or your life. Or go on a special adventure to find specific items, like a trip to the park to find things from nature, or a walk in your neighborhood to find things from your life

BOOKS

Nana's Big Surprise: The roosters have feathers on their tales from a bag of odds and ends someone gave me.

PAINT

Tempera, Acrylic, Oil, Gouache

HOW TO WORK WITH

I have been working with **acrylics** for over 15 years. They can be worked with like watercolors because they are water soluble, as in **Fiesta Feminina** or can be layered on since acrylics dry quickly. It's like building a color or a surface. Look closely at the table cloth in **My Diary From Here to There** on pages 4 and 5. See the lavender on the bottom layer with the other colors and patterns painted in layers on top. This is a good example of using under painting to give an inner glow or a richness to a surface. I have painted most of my books in acrylics.

Tempera paint is inexpensive and velvety. This is a great paint for simple color.

Oil paints dry slowly and are not water soluble. While they may not be ideal for the classroom, it is good to know a little about them. Frida Kahlo predominantly painted in oils. Look closely at her work. You can see how finely she could blend and layer. Oil paints are like butter. Marla Olmstead began painting with oils when she was four years old. Her work is large and amazing. So you are never too young to begin.

Gouache paints are water soluble. You can work with them like watercolors, but they are not transparent. They are opaque when dry.

BOOKS

My Colors, My World: I painted the entire book using acrylics.

Fiesta Feminina: Celebrating Women in Mexican Folktales: I used acrylics like watercolors.

The projects are generally best on paper that is at least 8 ½ x 11. However, larger paper provides more room for expression and is almost always preferable when available.

Black Paper loves oil pastels. It dramatically highlights the power and vibrancy of the colors.

Book Pages make an interesting back drop to a painting or drawing. Choose a special book to rip a page from to contribute to the story of the art. I always find really wonderful books abandoned on the streets or in thrift stores.

Watercolor Paper is my paper of choice for painting with acrylics and as a base for collage.

Newsprint Paper can come in large sizes and is great for big drawings in charcoal or chalk pastel. Sometimes you can get the leftover ends of large rolls from local newspapers. All of my books have paper as a base.

Colored Paper, Drawing Paper, Newsprint Paper, Watercolor Paper, Handmade Paper, Book Pages, Printed Paper, Tissue Paper, Tracing Paper, Black Paper, Photo Paper

Animal Poems of the Iguazu: I cut out colored paper of different textures and weights to create the environment. I used watercolor paper to paint the animals in acrylic paint.

BOOKS

Nana's Big Surprise: For much of the background and clothes of the characters, I printed photos on a matte or luster finish photo paper. A watercolor paper was used for the base.

Just Like Me: I copied a photo in black and white on cardstock at a copy shop and painted over it with acrylics.

I use **graphite pencils**, when I lay down a first drawing. I like to use a very hard lead like 4H because it leaves a very soft line. Many pencils across the world, and almost all in Europe, are graded on the European system using a continuum from "H" (for hardness) to "B" (for blackness), as well as "F" (for fine point). The standard writing pencil is graded HB. All of my books have some kind of drawing underneath.

Graphite Pencils, Colored Pencils, Watercolor Pencils, Pastel Pencils

Colored Pencils are one of my favorites. Many artists use a light touch and create a soft look using colored pencils. I layer them thick and heavy to create a dense, rich look.

Watercolor Pencils have the ease and control of drawing, apply a brush dipped in water afterwards to create a painted effect.

Pastel Pencils are found in art stores. These give the control and familiarity of a pencil but the color and texture of a soft pastel.

SCISSORS

Regular, Pinking Shears, Fancy Edged

HOW TO WORK WITH The sharper the **scissor** the finer the cut. Tiny very sharp scissors were used for cutting the paper for the water in *Animal Poems of the Iguazu*. I could whip around the small round edges to create the effect of splashing water. The trick, I found, is to move the paper and not the scissors.

Scissor Safety: I like sharp scissors. I believe it's valuable to teach from an early age how to handle any sharp utensil appropriately so that children can use any tool necessary. But I appreciate that many people do not teach this and that it may be more successful to use children's scissors in the classroom.

BOOKS In *Animal Poems of the Iguazu & Nana's Big Surprise*, I used all different sizes of scissors to cut out the paper, from very tiny to large scissors.

SIDEWALK CHALK

Old Favorite

HOW TO WORK WITH Use **sidewalk chalk** to create sidewalk murals with the whole class. Sidewalk chalk also works on brick walls or cement buildings. Use water squirters and big house brushes to create different effects with the chalk and have fun!

Being creative outside connects us to the bigger sweep of creativity in nature and gives more space to expand into our own expression. Working collaboratively on a mural in this setting supports community and provides a forum to practice respect for each other's contribution.

Take pictures to remember the work or just let the process of creating the art be what is taken away from the experience.

STICKERS

Handmade, Decoration

HOW TO WORK WITH Make your own **stickers** by drawing on precut stickers or blank mailing labels available in stationary or office supply stores. Or, use pre-made stickers to add dimension to your art.

BOOKS *Nana's Big Surprise:* I used rose and daisy stickers to accent Nana's shawl.

When I paint I always have a paint *towel* to dry my brush as I work. Old

TOWELS

kitchen towels or ripped t-shirts work great for this.

One towel per student is advisable, especially if you're working with paints a lot. Make sure you let them dry after using them so they do not mildew. Wash them separately after about 4-5 uses or depending on how fabulously well-used they become. Once washed, they will most likely remain stained. No problem. They're just for drying off brushes! I have had most of my towels for years.

Old Towels, T-shirts, Paper Towels

Alternatively, you can use paper towels.

Hard Cake Watercolors are a childhood classic. They are probably

WATERCOLORS

the easiest paints to have in the classroom. I will only mention a few techniques: (1) When you paint on dry paper, add a lot of water to the paint cake to create the transparent washes watercolors are great for, or use little water and create thick, dark colors. (2) Brush your paper with water first to create ethereal land, sky, or waterscapes. (3) Once dried go into the painting again and add drawings in more watercolor, pencils, even crayon or pastels. (4) Other effects can be created by sprinkling salt on watercolors as they are drying or sprinkling or spraying water on your watercolors once dried. Make sure you have someplace for them to dry flat. Since we usually print the photo portraits on a heavy cardstock for the CLAIMING FACE projects, watercolor washes can be used on these too.

Hard Cake or Tube

Watercolor Tubes are available in art stores. With these you have more control in mixing. It is also easier to paint them dark if desired because you can dip your brush directly into wet pigment from the tube.

Laughing Tomatoes and Other Spring Poems: here you can see

BOOKS

large washed areas that I let dry and then went back over to create patterns, like in the grass on the cover or the floor on Cinco de Mayo. You can also see the fine details created by thicker pigment in the facial features and hair.

IDEAS FOR MIXING MATERIALS:

Crayons and Watercolors

Cut Paper and Oil Pastels

Thick Markers and Color Pencils

Charcoal and Watercolors

TAKE THE MATERIALS FURTHER

Some materials are compatible because they are opposites like oil pastels and watercolors. The oil in the pastels repels the watercolors. This dynamic allows the two materials to remain separate while affecting each other. Imagine the different ways you can use them. If you lay down the oil pastels first, they will act like a border to hold the watercolors in place. If you paint with the watercolors first, they serve as a background and the oil pastels can be drawn on top. Experiment and imagine what other materials may be compatible. It is often because there's something opposite about them.

BOOKS *I Know the River Loves Me:* (Charcoal and Ink) I used charcoal to represent the girl because I wanted her appearance to be dramatic and stand out from the river. I used inks to create the environment. So much of the environment was the river and I wanted an art material that was in itself flow-y and watery. I chose inks instead of watercolors because I wanted both the girl and the river to be drawn and inks are more drawn than painted.

Nana's Big Surprise: (Cut Photos, Paint and Feathers) I love to paint, but I wanted to include the actual textures and colors of my world in this one. I photographed clothes and cloth, jewelry and statues. When I cut and glued them into the bigger painting I imagined that I was "painting" with photos.

Animals Poems of the Iguazu: (Cut Paper and Cut Paintings on Paper) In this book I painted the animals, then cut them out and treated them just like all the other cut paper to create the world of the rainforest. Here the "opposites" were cut paper and painted paper, but everything was paper.

MATERIAL VARIATIONS FOR PROJECTS

When working with the CLAIMING FACE projects, specific materials are recommended. However, always feel free to make any and all substitutions. Becoming familiar with the materials gives you more freedom and confidence to experiment. **A quick note:** oil pastels, chalk pastels and crayons can usually be interchanged. Charcoal can be exchanged for pencils.

MATERIALS COST MONEY!

Since the cost of art supplies can add up with a class of 30+ students, I have tried to keep art materials to a minimum. For example, provide each student with a small basic box of oil pastels of 6-12 colors and have a classroom set with 50 or more colors. Each student gets to choose 1-2 special colors from the larger box to add to their basic box. Or, the larger box can be set out during the project so that children can borrow colors from it as they work on their art. You can do this with many of the materials. Often you can find a local craft or art store with discounts for educators or special deals online. I have listed a few possibilities in the *Resources* at the back of the book.

ART MATERIALS Many materials can be found at the drugstore. Adjust your kits as much as you need, just make sure to have one!

ART MATERIALS CHECKLISTS

IDEAL STUDENT KIT

☐ Pencil

☐ Eraser

☐ Crayons: Box of 12-24 colors

☐ Oil Pastels: Box of 6-12 colors

☐ Markers: at least 2 colors

☐ Colored Pencils: 6-8 colors

☐ Scissors

☐ Box or Bag to hold and store materials (such as a zip-lock bag)

☐ Art board

☐ Box or Plastic container with lid for collecting found objects (such as a plastic yogurt container)

Other Fabulous Things to have on hand:

• Staples

• Pipe Cleaners

• Needle and Thread

• Hole Punch and Brads (which I love to use to make books or moveable doll self portraits)

EVERYONE IS AN ARTIST!

IDEAL CLASSROOM KIT

☐ Tape and/or Glue (stash of glitter glue) (set for each table)

☐ Crayons (Large box:64+)

☐ Oil pastels (Large box:50+)

☐ Chalk pastels (Large box: 48+)

☐ Colored pencils (Large box: 50+)

☐ Watercolor set; hardcake (2 per table of 8-16 colors)

☐ Brush (at least 1 for each student)

☐ Plastic covers for tables

☐ Containers for water (1 for every 2 students)

☐ Plastic lid or Styrofoam tray to use as a palette to mix colors (1 for each student)

☐ Art towel (1 for each student)

☐ Smock/Cover-up - shirt and possible art sleeves (1 for each student)

☐ Box of miscellaneous odds and ends

☐ Tracing paper

☐ Colored paper

☐ Newsprint

☐ Books to tear pages from

☐ Watercolor paper

☐ Sidewalk chalk (1 box per table)

☐ Huge brushes, water buckets, spray bottles

Working with Photographs

Several of the *Claiming Face* projects use photographs to explore a sense of self.

WHY PHOTOS?

I am not interested in teaching a child to draw a chair to look like a chair. I trust that they will develop and pursue greater and greater skill if that is important to them. In *Artistic Development* in *Chapter 5* there are some suggestions for ways to support students in pursuing just that. With this curriculum, I am interested in providing children with tools to know themselves and come face to face with their own creative power. I want to see them using their creative power to become stronger and see their lives, their self and the world as their works of art. So while I believe that the students will become more adept at drawing faces through this, it is not the goal.

I believe that we are strongly affected by our own image and by using it repeatedly we come to see and accept ourselves more deeply. Facing ourselves, while focusing our creative expression on ourselves, creates an association between our sense of self and the power of creativity. Creativity becomes a constant tool to explore, empower and express ourselves.

HOW TO CREATE PHOTOS

You will need some way to create black and white photos of your students. There are a number of ways to do this. Some are more expensive and time-consuming than others. I always recommend the most convenient, especially when first working with the curriculum. Choose what matches your style and accessibility best. **It is not necessary for the photos to be absolutely perfect or of the highest quality.** What is important is to have a likeness of each student to make art on.

Film camera. Purchase black & white film or develop regular film in black & white.

Disposable camera. Purchase a black & white film disposable camera or develop the film in black & white.

With both of these options you have the photo in hand and can take it to the copy shop, enlarge the images to fit 8 ½ x 11 and have them printed on the paper needed.

Digital camera. Either print black & white photos directly from a computer or order black & white photos from your digital files to enlarge and print at a copy shop.

Alternatively, copy any color photographs as black & white onto the paper needed. Or even copy and make art on the students' official school photos.

MORE FUN PROJECT IDEAS:

- Diorama for *Portrait of Self as Space or Place* project

- Quilt with *I Am Here Flags/ Hand Portrait* sewn together

- Mural or "Billboard" for the classroom telling a story

- Mobile that illustrates all the primary elements of a story or self

- A mask with an inside (who you are inside) and an outside (what you may show the world)

- Collaborative Art

- Listen to music and draw what it looks like on your photo, on your face

    the possibilities are endless......

Photo Frequency. If possible take photos twice during the school year, once toward the beginning of the school year like October and then again in the winter, like January/ February.

Staging the Photos. You want a plain background. If you don't have empty wall space available, tape up a large piece of white paper. Have the students come up one by one and stand in front of the paper facing you and the camera. I like to take at least two photos of each student. One that I call "regular" and one "wild." The regular one is the same as if they were looking in a mirror. Smile (or not) looking straight ahead. In the wild one they can do anything they like. Stick out their tongue, cross their eyes, look up, look down, frown, look like they are screaming or laughing or snarling. You name it. Make sure that their head is fully framed by the plain background in the photo view on your camera and only photograph their head and shoulders. Perfect!

Lighting. To flash or not to flash. This may be dependent on your individual circumstances. But it is highly likely that having a flash will simply make things easier and ensure a clear and bright enough image.

Printing. Use a heavy paper like cardstock, minimum 8½x11 or comparable, and white or cream in color. Print at home, a copy shop, or at school. If possible, look to see what projects you plan to use for the school year or semester and print up that many images of each student. Keep them on hand in a folder for easy access when needed. This gives you one less thing to think about when setting up a project. It will also give you the flexibility to pull out an art project whenever it seems like the best moment. Refer to *Chapter 9 Keys to Remember (pg. 182)* after the CLAIMING FACE projects for a quick list of the number of photos needed based on the project schedules.

Classroom Setup

I can adapt to make art in any amount of space available. I even take it camping. When I travel, I usually bring materials conducive to travel. At home, I condense my workspace by working with pens and colored pencils on small pieces of paper. When I am at my art studio, I can expand and work on large paintings with my acrylic paints laid out all the time. I try to make things physically as easy as possible. This makes art easy to sustain in my life and always accessible.

So, if you have plenty of space, wonderful. But, **if you have very limited space, you can still make art**. For a change of scenery, take a book to use as a "desk" and work outside. Draw in the library or the cafeteria or a playing field or at a museum or wherever you and your students have access to. Mix it up. Being mobile and flexible physically allows us to see creativity in as many different places in our life as possible.

CLASSROOM FLOW

Have a simple system to dispense the art materials to the class. Create a repetitive pattern. For example, first everyone gets out their art boards. Then everyone gets in line to get a box of pastels from the pastel container while the educator hands out paper and/or hand outs. Keep materials for art and clean up within reach of the students. Make sure students know where things are stored. Keeping all of the oil pastels in one labeled box and all of the chalk pastels in another makes storage, set up and clean up easier. Gather boxes with lids, like shoe boxes, or purchase fairly inexpensive plastic boxes with lids in varying sizes. Label them clearly, even mark with the material next to its name; a nice big smear of magenta next to the name OIL PASTELS.

Keep things predictable. This automatically gives the students a path to follow to set up for an art project and clean up as independently as possible. It is ideal if art materials are generally accessible to the students to work with when appropriate, for example, for free time. Having the boxes clearly labeled helps here too.

The primary goal is to create an **overall classroom flow that supports the students in being responsible and independent.** Involve students in every aspect of making art: set up, clean up, display and storage.

WORKSPACE

Everyone has their own style, but for the sake of keeping things flowing, create a classroom standard.

Desks. Generally, I assume students will work at their desks. Have them clear their desks off completely before getting out art materials. You may want to begin projects by covering the desk with plastic or paper, or by each student getting out their art board. Use large pieces of brown paper or plastic to cover the entire table. I often cut open garbage bags if I have to cover a large area or use heavy sheets of plastic from a fabric store. Both of these can be used over and over. Or, have the students just cover their area with either an individual square of plastic or an art board. Make sure everyone has all of the materials necessary for the project at hand.

Smocks. Besides covering up the desks for easier clean up, you may want to cover up the students. If you don't already have smocks for your classroom, gather the following from students, other teachers or thrift stores to wear over clothes: old shirts with a button front, t-shirts, or tank tops. Use a size or two larger than the students normally wear so that it can fit comfortably over clothes.

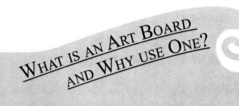

WHAT IS AN ART BOARD AND WHY USE ONE?

Having an art board is not necessary, but it is useful. You can keep a drawing you are working on for a long time taped to your board so it is always handy and ready to work on. You can also take your board anywhere you want to draw.

Art boards can be made out of many things. Purchase them from any art store, or make your own with easy to find materials:

• Any piece of wood, masonite, plastic

• Cardboard - for certain projects (although corrugated cardboard can leave grooves in your drawing)

• Tag board, heavy weight

I recommend tag board, the thickest and the cheapest you can find, usually at an art store, a paper store, or online. The color doesn't matter. Large pieces can be cut with a straight edge and a blade. A 9x12 Heavy Weight Tag Board is a good size and weight.

When you go adventuring into the world to make art, students can bring along their art board to use as a portable desk.
(View a picture of art boards on the adjacent page, Fig. 1)

Art Sleeves. These are my invention. I like to dress up, even if I'm working alone in my studio. I was always getting pencil and ink and glue and paint and everything all over my lovely sleeves. One day I cut up a pair of leggings and Voila! I slipped them over my sleeves and they took all the smudges and smears. Now I don't paint without them. I have two pair so I always have a spare. You can use leggings, tights, socks or long t-shirt sleeves. Snip, snip and you have your own art sleeves!

CLEAN UP

Leave enough time to clean up. Everyone is responsible for clean up. Art is laid out in a safe place to dry, tucked into portfolios or gathered by

Fig. 1-Art Boards and Art Sleeves

the educator. Materials are returned to their larger storage containers. Tools rinsed out and left to dry or stored. Table covers put away, the classroom returned to its formal state. Again, create a repetitive pattern to keep it predictable for greater flow.

Displaying Artists' Work

Something special happens when I publicly share my art. I used to be uncomfortable with it because part of me is very shy. But over time I learned that it makes me stronger to be seen. I am claiming face in community and affirming that I belong. I am here. I have also found that other people see themselves in my work and this creates reflection for them. When work is displayed with respect and shared with others, it affirms the importance of creating it and by extension, the value of the creative being who created it.

Sharing the art that comes out of working with the CLAIMING FACE projects is also part of the flow of the classroom. Creating an environment that supports sharing and speaking about art is discussed in greater length in *Presence in the Classroom* in *Chapter 4*.

Gallery. A specific area, like a designated board to serve as a "special" place where these projects are regularly displayed, is ideal. Name this space and display the title above. Some ideas are: *Who We Are, Our Gallery, Artist Gallery, I Am Here* or *EVERYONE IS AN ARTIST!*

Curator. Putting up and taking down art from the gallery space, with respect, could be a special task that rotates throughout the class. Define and describe it as the "curators" task.

Art Openings. Whenever possible, take the students' work up and out into the world to share with families, friends and even strangers. It is a great excuse for celebration. This could be within the school such as hallways, cafeteria, or library displays or more public spaces such as local cafes, museums, galleries, or the local library.

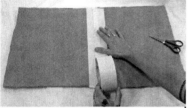

Fig.1⌐

Fig. 2⌐

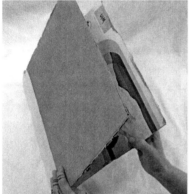

Fig. 3⌐

Fig. 4⌐

Fig. 5⌐

Fig. 6⌐

Storage

Art can pile up like crazy if you are working on it a lot. Have easy places for things to dry or be safely stored. Recall that for fragile art, such as projects made with pastels or charcoal, it is good practice to place an additional piece of paper or plastic over the artwork before storing. Alternatively you can use plastic wrap or thick plastic sheeting from a fabric store and cut pieces to fully wrap the piece. There are also plastic sleeves you can purchase at art stores.

Another option for a more permanent preservation is to use a fixative spray. Fixative is a permanent protective coating for sealing artwork, especially those created with charcoals, soft pastels, or pencils that can smear easily. It usually comes in an aerosol spray can. There is also a "workable fixative" that allows artists to go back into their drawing. If you go this route, make sure you buy a good quality fixative and use in a well ventilated area, preferably outdoors. Place artwork upright and spray 2-3 coatings evenly over the surface from a minimum of 2 feet away. Fixatives tend to darken the colors so be aware that this will likely alter the look of a finished piece.

For actual storage, use a large plastic or cardboard box like a file. Have a section for each student with a divider and their name on it. When work is ready to be stored, after a project is completed or has dried, they can find their name and put their work in their file. If you need more space or do not need to keep everything together, your students can make the super simple portfolio, photographed here and outlined on the following page, to keep track of all of their finished work themselves.

PORTFOLIO-RESPECT WHAT YOU'VE MADE

Purpose of Project:

Preserving art is a way to show respect for self, the work, and the creative process. If making art becomes a way that the young artist continues to work, then being able to look back at art made at different times can show development on multiple levels. Imagine how interesting it would be to have a portfolio of art for every year that you were growing up. Especially if much of the art was self-portraiture.

Process:

└A finished Portfolio decorated with *Frida Mirrors* created by students.

1. Place cardboard pieces next to each other on flat surface so that long sides are close enough to touch. *(Fig. 1)*

2. Tape along the line where the two pieces are touching, this will become the fold at the bottom of the portfolio. *(Fig. 2)*

3. Tape a strip of duct tape down again on either side of the initial strip to strengthen.

4. Turn entire portfolio over and do the same to the back side.

5. Now fold in half like a book, this is the body of your portfolio. *(Fig. 3)*

6. To make a handle, cut two piece of duct tape about 15 inches each in length.

7. Fold each piece in half length-wise, so that they tape onto themselves. *(Fig. 4)*

8. Place one on each side of portfolio like a handle and secure with duct tape. *(Fig. 5)*

9. Decorate madly!!!

10. Place all your wonderful art inside your new portfolio! *(Fig. 6)*

MATERIALS

• Two pieces of cardboard the same size--4inches wider in length and width as largest piece of art (for each student)

Teacher Tip: old boxes work great for this, if you can't collect enough yourself, consider finding cheap or even free ones on Craigslist.org for your city or ask local stores for a donation of their old packing boxes.

• Duct tape

Optional:

Single-Hole punch & string/ribbon

11. Additionally, you can have pieces of newsprint or tissue paper inside your portfolio to separate stored art. This is particularly useful for pastel and charcoal art.

12. *If desired*, you can also punch holes near the top middle on each side of the portfolio (near the handles). Then add string or ribbon to allow the portfolio to be tied closed as an extra precaution to prevent art from falling out.

Keys to Remember from Chapter 7:

Using the Materials

- If you're getting dirty, you know you're making art.
- Using materials like Charcoal and Oil Pastels make a big difference in instilling confidence in children that they are artists.
- Familiarize yourself with the materials for more freedom and confidence to explore.
- Much of the art in the projects is linked to art in a related book, combining literacy with art.

Working with Photographs

- Choose the photo style most convenient to you.
- Photos don't have to be perfect, just need a good likeness of each student.
- Use a flash and shoot only head and shoulders against a plain background.
- Two shots per student, one regular and one wild.
- Take photos twice a year if possible, once in October and again in January/February.
- Copy and store as many photos as you need for the school year or semester to make project preparation simpler.
- Always print on a heavy paper like cardstock.

Classroom Set Up

- Support flow through simple and predictable set up and clean up practices.
- Involve students in every aspect of making art, set up, clean up, display and storage.
- Have accessible art materials to use during students' free time.
- Store art materials in reach of students in clearly marked boxes.
- Keep clean up easy by covering the desks or have an art board for each student.

Display

- Gallery: have a specially designated area to serve as the self-portrait gallery.
- Curator: taking down and putting up new work is a special job.
- Art openings: share work in larger and larger communities.
- Treat work respectfully.

Storage

- Have safe places for things to dry if wet.
- Cover art made with pastels or charcoal with an extra sheet of paper or plastic before storing.
- Have a place to store completed work.
- Create a portfolio.

CHAPTER 8

Books: Behind the Story

*I*n 1994, at my first art opening in San Francisco, I met Harriet Rohmer, the founder of Children's Book Press. Children's Book Press is identified as *"the country's first publisher to focus exclusively on quality multicultural and bilingual literature for children."* Harriet preferred to work with actual artists from the same communities as the authors. She says, *"When a child opens a book and sees someone like herself or himself, it has the power to change that child's life and create an ongoing relationship to reading."* When Harriet asked me if I was interested in making art for a children's book, I felt as though I had come home. But home to a place I never knew existed.

In this chapter you will find the basic information about the books I have either illustrated and/ or authored up to the year 2010. Included are some of the stories behind the art to give a fuller understanding of what is in the imagery and the process. Hopefully, this will serve as a resource to inspire children to look deeper into these books and all of the books in their lives.

I, Francisco Alarcon, and Amada Irma Perez, all use our books to model the importance of self reflection. In telling our personal stories, not only do we hope to provide resonant reflections for children, we also hope to inspire and support children in telling their own stories and creating their own reflections.

Anthologies

Note on all books: All books can be read out loud to younger students or more deeply engaged with for older students. Book synopses have been taken from the publisher's websites.

JUST LIKE ME

Stories and Self-Portraits by Fourteen Artists

Synopsis: With vivid colors and emotion, the artists gathered in this collection present stunning self-portraits and personal statements. Intimate, serious, and funny, their stories explore their inspirations, their ethnic backgrounds, how they see themselves, and what their art means to them. Through stories, paintings, and childhood photographs, these fourteen artists open their hearts and invite us to enter into their worlds. With honesty and encouragement, they offer hope for aspiring young people who dream of becoming artists—just like them.

Behind the Story: I wanted to tell a magical story about something that happened to me as a very young person. So I decided that I wanted to mix a very real image of myself with the fantastic element of the story. I went to an old photo booth and took photos of myself with pencils and brushes in my hair pretending to paint my heart. Then I printed it onto heavy cardstock paper in black and white to paint. I accidentally laid the photo on the printer bed crooked and when the print came out the other side it was lopsided. Perfect! I decided. I wrote things that I love around the image, one of which is polka dots. When I ask kids if they can still see the light from the story coming out of my heart, most of them yell out "YES!" This thrills me.

RELATED PROJECTS

1. *Photo Self-Portrait, pg.140*
2. *What No One Can See Portrait   pg.172*
3. *All of Me Portrait/Portrait/ Portrait/Portrait   pg.180*
4. *I Frame Myself-Word Window   pg.166*
5. *Boss of Me Portrait,pg.154*
6. *Wildest Self Collage,pg.134*

AGES: 6 & UP

Edited by Harriet Rohmer, 1997; English; Hardcover 32 pages
Published by Children's Book Press, San Francisco, CA
Awards: California Readers Elementary California Collection; Small Press Book Award Finalist

HONORING OUR ANCESTORS

Stories and Self-Portraits by Fourteen Artists

Synopsis: This remarkable book brings together fourteen outstanding and diverse artists to honor the ancestors who most touched their lives and to pay playful tribute to the influential and loving people who came before them. Through stories, art, and photographs, Honoring Our Ancestors will inspire children and their families to gain strength from the past as they ask themselves, "Who do I honor?"

AGES: 6 & UP

Edited by Harriet Rohmer, 1999; English; Hardcover 32 pages
Published by Children's Book Press, San Francisco, CA
Awards: Parent's Choice Silver Honor Winner; Skipping Stones Honor Award Winner

RELATED PROJECTS

1. *Myself as Ancestor, pg.158*

ON MY BLOCK
Stories and Paintings by Fifteen Artists

Synopsis: Is there a part of your block that you especially love to explore? A place in your house or another country that holds a special memory? A far away spot you've heard about that excites your imagination? Children's Book Press asked fifteen exceptional fine artists to portray, in words and pictures, the places that are most special to them. On My Block is the remarkable result. The fifteen paintings and stories within ask you to ponder the places that comprise your world. What's on your block, down your street, in another country, that makes up who you are?

Behind the Story: I chose to share the empty page as my favorite place to explore. I framed the story in relation to discovering "real" art materials waiting for me after coming out of a coma.

AGES: 6 & UP

Edited by Dana Goldberg, 2007; English; Hardcover 32 pages
Published by Children's Book Press, San Francisco, CA

RELATED PROJECTS

1. *On My Block,*   *pg.160*

Written By Maya

MY COLORS, MY WORLD

Synopsis: Maya longs to find brilliant, beautiful color in her world. But when the wind blows, desert sand covers everything, and turns her whole neighborhood the color of dust. With the help of a feathered friend, Maya searches high and low to find the colors in her world. And she does—in the vibrant purple of her Mama's flowers, the juicy green of a prickly cactus, the hot pink clouds at sunset, and the shiny black of her Papi's hair.

Behind the Story: The understory in this book is that the girl is looking for herself after an event that has changed everything in her world. Her world has gone flat and colorless. In looking for color in her world, she actually finds her own reflection and beauty in the world around her.

The opening scene shows huge winds practically blowing the whole world over. Those winds felt like ancient, unseeing forces. If you turn the book over you can see faces on the windy swirls. They are based on Eccentric Flints used as ritual tools in Meso-America. They have lips and noses, but no eyes.

RELATED PROJECTS

1. *Emotions of Color,* *pg.148*
2. *Self-Portrait as Space or Place*   *pg.170*

AGES: 4-8 YEARS

Written by Maya Christina Gonzalez, 2007
Bilingual in English & Spanish; Hardcover 24 pages
Published by Children's Book Press, San Francisco, CA
<u>Awards:</u> **2008 Pura Belpré Illustrator Honor Award; Texas 2x2**
       Reading List Selection; Texas Library Association;
       Criticas Magazine's Best Children and YA Books;
       International Latino Book Awards, Best Children's
       Picture Book, Bilingual, 2nd Place

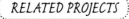

I KNOW THE RIVER LOVES ME

Synopsis: Listen, can you hear the river calling you? Rushing and bubbling, splashing or still, the river has so much to teach us. Whenever little Maya visits the river, the river jumps up to greet her. It cools her down when the summer sun is too hot, and keeps her company in the quiet of winter. The river takes care of Maya and Maya takes care of the river.

Behind the Story: One of my good friends is the Yuba River in eastern California. I go to visit her every year. We spend time and play and relax. One summer, I was sitting with her and she began telling me a story. I listened. I didn't know if it was a children's story or an adult story. I just paid attention and held it in my mind. When I got back to the city, my friend Dana called from Children's Book Press and asked if I could do a book for them and if I had a story. I laughed out loud. *"Yes!"* I said. *"The river just told me one."* She must have known I was going to need one.

RELATED PROJECTS

1.I Know the River Loves Me
pg. 176

AGES: 4-8 YEARS

Written by Maya Christina Gonzalez, 2009
Bilingual in English & Spanish; Hardcover 24 pages
Published by Children's Book Press, San Francisco, CA

Books with Francisco Alarcón

LAUGHING TOMATOES

and other Spring Poems

Synopsis: From the imagination of poet Francisco X. Alarcón comes this playful and moving collection of twenty poems about spring: welcoming the morning sun, remembering his grandmother's songs, paying tribute to children working in the fields, and sharing his dream of a world filled with gardens.

Behind the Story: I created a character that was Francisco and one that was me to play inside of Francisco's poems. I also included all of my animals at the time! Who am I? Clue: I love polka dots.

Secret: Look at the poem with the same name as the book. If you look very closely you can see someone winking at you. Usually children who meet me are the only ones who I tell and it's proof that they have met me. I have only met one child in hundreds who claims to have found it before I told her.

AGES: 6 & UP

Written by Francisco X. Alarcon, 1997;
Bilingual in English & Spanish; Hardcover/Paperback 32 pages
Published by Children's Book Press, San Francisco, CA
Awards: **Pura Belpré Honor Award; National Parenting**
Publications Gold Medal Award; Riverbank Review
"Children's Books of Distinction" Finalist

FROM THE BELLYBUTTON OF THE MOON

and other Summer Poems

Synopsis: With a poet's magical vision, Francisco takes us back to his childhood, when he traveled with his family to Mexico to visit his grandmother and other relatives.

AGES: 6 & UP

Written by Francisco X. Alarcon, 1998;
Bilingual in English & Spanish; Paperback 32 pages
Published by Children's Book Press, San Francisco, CA
**Awards: Pura Belpré Author Honor, Américas Award
Commended List; Cooperative Children's Book
Center Choice; Skipping Stones Honor Award; School
Library Journal Starred Review; California Readers,
Elementary California Collection**

ANGELS RIDE BIKES

and other Fall Poems

Synopsis: In *Angels Ride Bikes*, Francisco Alarcón invites us to experience autumn in Los Angeles—the City of the Angels—where dreams can come true. In the poet's whimsical imagination, mariachis play like angels, angels ride bikes, and the earth dances the cha-cha-chá. Francisco celebrates the simple joys and trials of everyday life: a visit to the outdoor market, the arrival of the ice cream vendor, the first day of school. He honors his family and pays tribute to his mother, who taught him that with hard work and education he could realize his dreams.

Behind the Story: I noticed children talking about cheating when making art. I decided that I was going to try to cheat as much as possible in a book. It seemed that children thought that tracing was a big NO-NO, so I wanted to basically emulate tracing for an entire book. I took black and white photos of different people I knew in California and Oregon. I posed them like the characters in the book. The two people in Tooth Magic, page 20-21 never met. The boy lived in Oregon and the dentist was my actual dentist in San Francisco. I enlarged the photos to fit my paintings and printed them on heavy paper. I then glued them onto my drawing and painted over the entire thing as if the pieces were just part of the drawing. I made sure that if you looked closely you could see where I glued things down. I didn't try to hide it. In fact, I hoped that children would see those lines and wonder why they were there. The ice cream man on page 8 is my father. He's actually standing in his driveway in Oregon holding a twig. He doesn't have a mustache like that. Can you see the lines that cross his chest and belly? Can you tell which character is me? I'll give you a clue. I love to cheat, I mean teach!

RELATED PROJECTS

1. *Making Face Puzzle,* pg.130
2. *Cheat Please!,* pg.146

AGES: 6 & UP

Written by Francisco X. Alarcon, 1999;
Bilingual in English & Spanish; Paperback 32 pages
Published by Children's Book Press, San Francisco, CA
**Awards: Notable Book for a Global Society Award Winner,
Américas Award Commended Title;
National Parenting Publication Award Gold Award**

IGUANAS IN THE SNOW
and other Winter Poems

Synopsis: In this collection of seasonal poetry, poet Francisco X. Alarcón and artist Maya Christina Gonzalez invite us to celebrate winter—by the seashore, in the magic city of San Francisco, and in the ancient redwood forests of the Sierras.

Behind the Story: I grew up in California and I live in San Francisco, so this book was very familiar to me. In fact, some of the things I painted for this book I can see just by looking out of my window.

AGES: 6 & UP

Written by Francisco X. Alarcon, 2001;
Bilingual in English & Spanish; Paperback 32 pages
Published by Children's Book Press, San Francisco, CA
Awards: Pura Belpré Honor Award;
Americas Award Commended List

ANIMAL POEMS OF THE IGUAZÚ

Synopsis: In the magical rainforest of the Iguazú National Park, butterflies are the multicolored flowers of the air. Great dusky swifts watch over the park, and the untamed spirits of jaguars roam the jungle. Following the Amerindian oral tradition, award-winning Chicano poet Francisco X. Alarcón lets the animals of the Iguazú speak for themselves in their own soaring, roaring, fluttering voices, and the resulting poems are as urgent as they are beautiful and humorous.

Behind the Story: When I began making the art for this book, I asked if I could eliminate the humans, except as animals themselves. I love the poems being from the animal's perspective. It allows me to enter into their experience. I wanted my medium to be familiar to children. I ask children if they love to "cut and paste." And then tell them that's how I made this book. Look closely at how the environments are all cut paper. This was hard work. The animals are also cut paper but they are painted first. I love animals. Painting them was a sign of respect and focus for me. I created a paper world on each page for the painted animals to move in and out of. Before starting the art for the book, I watched videos online of the Iguazu falls to see how the water moved. There were hilarious videos of visitors going in boats under the falls. To me, they were like the animals, playing and having fun. This is why they are the only humans I paint in the book, shown on page 22.

RELATED PROJECTS

1. Animal Self-Portrait, pg. 136
2. I Know the River Loves Me
pg. 176

AGES: 6 & UP

Written by Francisco X. Alarcon, 2008;
Bilingual in English & Spanish; Hardcover 32 pages
Published by Children's Book Press, San Francisco, CA
Awards: Notable Books for a Global Society Selection,
Américas Award Commended Title

Books with Amada Irma Pérez

MY VERY OWN ROOM

Synopsis: Five little brothers, two parents, and a house full of visiting relatives make Amada feel crowded. She loves her family, but how can she get a little space of her own? Her loving and understanding family works together to turn a small storage space into her very own room.

Behind the Story: Crayons and pastels are like cousins. I created a book using oil pastels because I could use it as an example in the classroom. I believe children should use the same materials that artists use. Oil pastels are a perfect fit for children used to handling crayons.

AGES: 6 & UP

Written by Amada Irma Perez, 2000;
Bilingual in English & Spanish; Hardcover/Paperback 32 pages
Published by Children's Book Press, San Francisco, CA
Awards: **Tomás Rivera Mexican American Children's Book Award, Américas Award Honorable Mention, Parent's Guide to Children's Media "Outstanding Achievement in Books"**

RELATED PROJECTS

1. *Self-Portrait as Space or Place*   pg.170

MY DIARY FROM HERE TO THERE

Synopsis: One night, young Amada overhears her parents whisper of moving from Mexico to the other side—to Los Angeles, where greater opportunity awaits. As she and her family make their journey north, Amada records her fears, hopes, and dreams for their lives in the United States in her diary. How can she leave her best friend behind? What if she can't learn English? What if her family never returns to Mexico?

From Juárez to Mexicali to Tijuana to Los Angeles, Amada learns that with her family's love and her belief in herself, she can make any journey and weather any change—here, there, anywhere.

AGES: 6 & UP

Written by Amada Irma Perez, 2002;
Bilingual in English & Spanish; Hardcover/Paperback 32 pages
Published by Children's Book Press, San Francisco, CA
Awards: **Américas Award Commended Title
Pura Belpré Honor Award**

RELATED PROJECTS

1. *Map of Me*   pg.156

NANA'S BIG SURPRISE

Synopsis: Nana's move from Mexico should be a joyous occasion. But this summer Nana is coming to California because Tata, beloved husband and abuelo, has died. Amada and her five brothers hope to cheer her up with a surprise—a coop full of fluffy yellow chicks, just like the ones Nana raised with Tata in Mexico. But no matter how hard everyone tries to make Nana feel better, it seems like nothing can bring a smile to her face. That is, until one day the chicks reveal a surprise of their own.

Behind the Story: I took almost 1000 photos for this book of my clothes, jewelry and miscellaneous items. I had to learn how to use my friend's professional digital camera, download the pictures, use Photoshop and print them. Then I had to learn how to collage photos into a painting. This one was a big adventure! Initially I wanted to do collage to make it an easier process for me. I had already put this book on hold for three years because I became extremely ill. But I had a relatively miraculous healing. And with my fabulously expanding newfound health, what was initially intended to make things easier for "sick-me," became a lesson in complete and total extravagance and celebration for "healthy-me." I had been basically housebound for 3 years and so all of the textures and colors of my intimate world were loaded with richness and meaning to me. When I began working on the art for this book, I did huge photo shoots in my bedroom. It was a very intuitive process. As I photographed piece of clothing after piece of clothing, things like keys and Milagros started landing on different pieces. As the collages progressed I realized the keys were part of the children. They helped open the grandmother's heart. In the last spread there is one last image of keys. They are no longer carried about by the children. Now they rest in the ground and are part of the pattern of the earth. I used heart Milagros to document the grandmother's heart journey through grief. Look how the heart moves through the imagery. It is sticking out of her suitcase on page 9. By the last page, the heart is part of the cloth of her dress. Her shawl also serves as a symbol of her passage. It transforms from something heavy to hide under to wide wings to dance with and more and more flowers blooming on it.

My Interpretation of the Story: I loved the sense of time and the depth of this book and that it was a true story. ALL of those chicks turning out to be roosters made me think it was the spirit of the grandfather coming through to make the grandmother laugh. That's why at the end, she is hugging a photo of the grandfather while looking out the window at a rooster.

RELATED PROJECTS

1. *Symbol of Myself,* pg. 150
2. *Tell a Tale Without Words* pg. 174

AGES: 6 & UP

Written by Amada Irma Perez, 2007;
Bilingual in English & Spanish; Hardcover 32 pages
Published by Children's Book Press, San Francisco, CA
Awards: **International Latino Book Awards; Best Children's Picture Book, Bilingual, 2nd Place; Américas Award Commended Title; Tejas Star Book Award Finalist**

Books with Others

PRIETITA AND LA LLORONA

Synopsis: Ever since she can remember, Prietita has heard frightening stories about la Llorona—the legendary ghost woman who steals children at night. One day, when Prietita goes in search of the missing herb that can help cure her mother's illness, she becomes lost in the woods. Suddenly she hears a distant crying sound and sees flashes of white in the trees. Could it be the ghost woman from her grandmother's stories?

Behind the Story: The classic folktale of La Llorona is re-envisioned. Usually a story to frighten children, in this version the little girl, Prietita is remarkably brave and in tune with the animals and La Llorona is a spirit that guides her through the dark. Here are two amazing female characters, challenging an old tale.

RELATED PROJECTS

1. *Animal Self-Portrait, pg.136*
2. *Courage Portrait, pg. 164*

AGES: 6 & UP

Written by Gloria Anzaldúa, 1996;
Bilingual in English & Spanish; Paperback 32 pages
Published by Children's Book Press, San Francisco, CA
Awards: Americas Honor Award; Notable Book for a Global Society Award Winner, Smithsonian Notable Book

FIESTA FEMININA

Synopsis: Travel to lush Mexican forests, amidst tall mountains and rushing rivers to discover tales of the many heroines of Mexico. The eight stories in this collection capture the noble beauty of the women of Mexican folk tales.

AGES: 6 & UP

Retold By: Mary-Joan Gerson, 2001;
Bilingual in English & Spanish; Hardcover 32 pages
Published by Barefoot Books, Cambridge, MA
Awards: American Folklore Society's Aesop Prize 2001 Parent's Choice Recommended List 2001; Booklist Editor's Choice; Booklist Top Ten Children's Books On Women's History

RIGBY, CRYSTAL LAKE, IL

2001 "What Fine Gardeners"
1998 "Face Toward the Sky"
1996 "I Come From Two Lands"
1996 "The Crying Mountain"

SCOTT FORESMAN ADDISON WESLEY, GLENVIEW, IL

1999 "Amigos Inseparables" by Nicholosa Mohr for Reading 2000

KEYS TO REMEMBER FROM CHAPTER 8:

- *Just Like Me:* An unexplainable experience about light and the heart.

- *On My Block:* Recovery from a serious accident and the love of art that came with that experience.

- *My Colors, My World:* Finding color in the world after an experience has turned the world colorless. Turn the book upside down to see the blind faces on the wind swirls.

- *I Know the River Loves Me:* The river told me the story.

- *Laughing Tomatoes and Other Spring Poems:* There's a secret hidden in the art on the Laughing Tomato poem.

- *Angels Ride Bikes and Other Fall Poems:* Look for the lines in the art where I glued down the photos. Can you cheat in art?

- *Animal Poems of the Iguazu:* The animals were painted as a sign of respect. The rest of the book is made of cut paper to make the environments for the animals.

- *My Very Own Room:* See how to use oil pastels by looking at the art.

- *Nana's Big Surprise:* Look for the keys and how the heart moves and the shawl transforms throughout the art of the book.

Pause......

Pause for a moment and become aware of your breath. Feel your chest rise and fall. Feel your weight upon your chair. Let your body rest down. Feel the chair support your full body, your bones, your muscles, your organs. Notice your legs, your back, your arms, your neck. Notice your mind. *Are there thoughts in your head?* Notice the energy in your head, your jaw, your ears, your mouth, your eyes.

Now using your imagination, see a circle around you as wide as possible. It may encompass the entire building you are in or simply the room you are in. Sense the shape of that space, the architecture, the structural support, the materials encompassed in this large circle.

Now imagine a medium sized circle. If your first visual was the whole building, perhaps this next visual is the room you're in. If you imagined the room first, perhaps this next visual is the table or desk you're sitting at.

Pause in the space of this middle circle. Notice the air that you're breathing in this space. In and then out. Just sitting here, reading and breathing, you are affecting the air around you. Your breath however subtle is affecting the air current, temperature and quality. Just keep sitting here, breathing. Stop reading for a moment and purposefully don't DO anything. If a thought comes up, notice it, but don't think it.

∞• ◇•∞• ◇•∞• ◇•∞• ◇•∞• ◇•∞• ◇•∞• ◇•∞ **PAUSE** ∞• ◇•∞• ◇•∞• ◇•∞• ◇•∞• ◇•∞• ◇•∞• ◇•∞

Now imagine a circle in the central core of your body. Breathe. Notice what kind of circle you've created in the center of your body. *Does it exist in your chest? Or does it run like a column down the center of your body? Maybe it's in your head? Your heart? Your belly?* Specifically locate the core circle you've created. Now remember the first large circle you created, then return to the core circle within you. Practice for a moment going back and forth between noticing the large circle and the core circle. Large circle, core circle. *Are you aware of passing through the middle circle?* Imagine that as you breathe in, you begin at the core circle and as you breathe out, you expand out to the large circle. You may notice that you need to take a deep breath or yawn as you play with your imagination like this.

When you feel ready, pick up your pencil or pen and draw the 3 concentric circles that you imagined.

Use the following page to draw your circles........

Draw it! Claim it!

Draw it! Claim it!

Draw it! Claim it!

Reflect

1 We are always growing when we are young. Expanding. Becoming something bigger that we cannot understand until we arrive. Pretend for a moment that (even though you are a grown up) there is still a significant amount of growth for you to experience. Knowing this, how would your perspective of your self be different? How would your perspective of your life possibly be different?

2 What area of yourself or your life can you imagine becoming bigger or more expanded? How would this affect you? Your life? Your relationships? Your work? Your world?

3 Imagine for a moment that as a result of doing the Imagine exercise above you were now bigger in some way. What's the first thing you would do as a bigger or more expanded self?

4 What would your world look like if, as this bigger self, you knew in every way that you are an artist? There's not a right or a wrong way? You are courageous?

5 Consider this as you either do the following projects yourself and/or share the projects with your students.

A Pause before the Process

Now you have gathered a sense of the philosophy and practice from *Part One* coupled with information about art materials, and books in *Part Two*. This will not only support you doing or sharing the projects in *Part Three*, it will also support your understanding of the underlying meaning and purpose of the curriculum in a broader context.

The *Imagine* Exercises and *Reflect* Questions are just for you. They are a practice in presence and a step toward increasing your use of your imagination and experience in relation to the philosophy. Each of us has a different way that we come to our knowing. I hope to engage you in as many ways of knowing as possible. This naturally expands and deepens your understanding and experience. It also supports the relocating of who sees you to the inside. You begin to see more of yourself internally and begin to base your sense of knowing yourself on your own internal criteria.

As an educator, the more you personally understand the intent behind the curriculum and can practice it, the stronger you will be in yourself and in your classroom. This curriculum is for you first. You are the artist at the core.

The Shape of the Curriculum/Inside Outside

The concentric circles of the diagram to the right represent the shape of the curriculum and a model of presence. The whole circle is divided in half. The lower half contains 3 levels of internal or *Inside* experience. The upper half contains 3 levels of physical or *Outside* experience.

The outer most circle for *Inside* contains *Part One* which supports the internal experience through information about philosophy and practicing presence.

The outer most circle for *Outside* contains *Part Two* which supports the physical experience through information about art materials and books.

The middle circle for *Inside* directly supports the artist through the distillation of the philosophy into **THE 3 RULES**. The middle circle for *Outside* directly engages the artist through the 26 projects of CLAIMING FACE.

Finally, the center circle holds both the *Inside* and *Outside* of the artist, acknowledging the whole person through the internal and external experience.

"you are the artist at the core."

This is the shape of the curriculum. It is also a built-in model of presence. Like in the *Imagine Centering* exercise *(pg. 113)* in which you move back and forth between an inner awareness and an outer awareness, you practice holding multiple levels of experience simultaneously. Presence means bringing as much attention as possible to your experience, the inside and the outside. Our goal is to be able to accomplish the task at hand, while being aware of our inner experience no matter what it is. The boy in the story who kept repeating *"I can't, I can't"* is a good example. He was frozen physically until his internal experience was brought into awareness. Then he found that he had enough room for those feelings, which freed him up to be physically present enough to continue creating art. Both his internal experience (having difficult feelings) and his external experience (the self-portrait project) could exist at the same time. This illustrates how, embedded in the nature of the curriculum, is a slow-building internal development of presence, linked to creativity, in service to reflection. The whole artist is supported inside, outside and through process. Find yourself at the center of the diagram. This puts you on the same path that boy took. He taught me that:

ART IS ALWAYS AN ACT OF COURAGE.

"Presence begins small with oneself in the moment."

"Here and now."

PART 3

PROCESS

Beautiful art
will be made,
but what is truly
important,
more than the creation,
is the act of creating.

Art will fade, but the
power and strength
and self-knowing that
you experience will
always be yours
to carry with you.

This is the point of
engaging with the
creative process.

This is life.

*Reflect, express, explore, empower, expand and
become more free*

"Creativity is different all the time."

Chapter 9

Claiming Face Projects

Every step counts. Philosophies, Rules, Presence, Materials, Books, everything has lead to the CLAIMING FACE projects. The projects are the next step and provide form for the process. This is how we engage. Continuing on this path will lead you deeper into creativity and closer to knowing self. Along the way you and your students will, reflect, express, explore, empower, expand and become more free through the creative process and self-portraiture. Each step makes the next one possible. There are many steps beyond these. The projects are just the present ones in a life long process.

As much depth and support as possible has been provided on the journey here. That continues. As you journey through the projects, *Chapters 7 & 8* are specifically designed for easy reference for the materials and related books specified in the projects. The six project categories: **Reflection, Express, Explore, Empower, Expand,** and **Freedom,** serve to familiarize you with the nature and overall intent of each of the projects. Additionally, the project pages themselves, are not only informative, but laid out to function as a journal for you to track both your personal experience doing the projects as well as your experience of the project in the classroom. Please remember the *THE 3 RULES* and have as much fun as absolutely possible!

> *Rule #1: Everyone is an artist.*
>
> *Rule #2: There is never a right or wrong way to make art.*
>
> *Rule #3: Art is always an act of courage.*

Overview of Projects

All 26 CLAIMING FACE projects on the following pages are laid out in the same manner. If you recall from Chapter 1, each is divided into the *Purpose of the Project*, *Prep*, if any work is required to get the project ready for your class, the *Materials* needed, *Process* to guide students, and any related *Books*. Also included are step-by-step photographs and room to take notes about what happened, what did and didn't work, and any other ideas. The projects in the photos are intentionally left simple in order to leave as much room as possible for your own (and your students') creative power to rise up. The photos serve to illustrate the *process* but NOT to be examples of how the projects should look.

PROCESS. The *Process* steps are written in a way to easily bring each project into the classroom as a guided exercise. The initial steps usually help you set up the project, either physically or in words. The steps following *"Guide Artists in the following steps:"* have kept the "you" pronoun to make it more personally relevant. This also allows you to simply read the process out loud to your students should time be limited.

SYMBOLS. The symbols at the top right corner relate to the 6 project categories (*see table on pg. 125*) and whether it is part of the **Fundamentals Schedule** described in more detail in *Time and Schedule*. Watch for the clock symbol that indicates some prep is necessary. Project Prep is based on a class size of 30 students. Some project prep may be more involved than others indicated by the addition of a **plus sign**. Also, the camera and copy symbols indicate when you will either need photographs of your students and/or a trip to the copy shop. Throughout the projects I give examples from my own work with students and what I have learned. You can identify these tips and advice by the rose symbol. Review the symbols legend (*pg. 124*) for a quick overview of the symbols you're likely to encounter in this chapter and how they correspond to the projects.

MATERIALS AND BOOKS. How to use the different materials listed for each project is covered in the *Chapter 7, Materials, Display, and Storage*. Also, refer to *Chapter 8, Books: Behind the Story*, to learn more about the books associated with each project. The related books add more depth and experience to the project's purpose. I use the books as a way to ground the art experience, involve literacy, and create external reflection. You may want to read the recommended book(s) with your students before doing the project. Look closely at the art and investigate with your students how this art relates to the project. While this curriculum is rooted in my work and my books, please use whatever books you like to work with.

When all of the resources are used it creates a multi-layered experience that encourages multiple ways of knowing and thinking. How to speak about and share with others what has been created is explored in detail in *Chapter 4, Presence in Practice*.

TIME AND SCHEDULE

Each project generally takes **40 minutes to one hour for set up (including instruction), creation and clean up**. However, some projects can be expanded or taken in pieces, see more ideas to the right for variations on time.

Since it may not be possible for you to dedicate time to projects every day or every week, two project schedules have been provided (*page 127*). The **Fundamentals Schedule** allows for a monthly focus to integrate this in with other art or projects. The extended CLAIMING FACE **Full Schedule** provides a deeper engagement through weekly art projects. The subsequent CLAIMING FACE project pages (*pgs. 130-181*) follow the order of this list.

Using the schedules and project categories as guides, you can determine what will work best for your class. If time is limited, even committing 20 minutes a day to a project would provide consistent exposure. Projects do not have to be perfect or brought to the point where they can all be displayed. You can even repeat projects. We are not focused on product as much as process and experience.

VARIATIONS ON TIME

Frida Mirror: Study Frida's life as an artist, read books about Frida or her husband Diego Rivera, research Mexico where she lived, as well as completing the project. (This in-depth study can be done for many of the projects that are highlighted with the two asterisks on the project schedules- pg. 127)

Projects like THE 3 RULES signs: Work on for 15-20 minutes at a time, taking the whole week to complete.

Wildest Self and Tell a Tale Without Words projects: Take in steps; first day gather images, second day cut them out, third day do any necessary drawing or coloring, fourth day glue images into piece, fifth day add any special elements or final touches.

PROGRESSION

I have progressed the curriculum schedules to specifically build upon experience and the effects of the different projects. There is a momentum created as the year goes on that can support you and your students to embody what is in the philosophy. If at all possible it is best to do the full schedule.

VERY IMPORTANT: YOU are the artist in the classroom. Always follow your own direction and intuition regarding all of the projects. These are purely guidelines and are meant to support you and never bind you.

SYMBOLS LEGEND:

Familiarize yourself with the following symbols that you will encounter as you work with the projects. Also get acquainted with the 6 project category symbols on the following page.

Fundamentals Schedule
identifies projects that are part of the shorter monthly schedule

Project Prep Required
based on class size of 30; a PLUS sign indicates more involved prep

Materials for Project
corresponds to *Using The Materials* in *Ch. 7*

Books Associated with Project
corresponds to *Ch. 8, Books: Behind the Story*

Photos of Students needed
corresponds to *Working with Photographs* in *Ch. 7, pgs. 96-97*

Copies needed
handouts, photos, etc. usually onto a heavy cardstock

Maya Tip
tips, tricks, examples from my work in the classroom

Teacher Tip
tips to make the project run smoother

Project Categories

There are six project categories:

Reflection, Express,
Explore, Empower,
Expand, Freedom,

Each category describes a particular experience created by doing the project. For example, *Reflection* projects allow children to see themselves clearly in their art, thereby creating their own reflection. The categories, their resulting experience and the associated projects are listed in the table to the right (*pg. 125*). Recall that each of *THE 3 RULES* is further solidified by their specific categories and respective projects (*review table on pg. 74*).

Planning Tools

The next 3 pages provide various project lists and schedules to assist you in finding what will be the most fruitful for your class. Projects with, *photo*, listed next to the title indicate that these projects will use a copy of a student's photograph as a base. Refer to *Chapter 7* in the section titled, *Working with Photographs*. Projects with, *handout*, listed next to the title use one of the handouts provided in the *Resources* at the back of the book and require copies being made for your students. Refer to the *Keys to Remember* (*pg. 182*) at the end of this chapter for a quick list of the minimum copies needed based on the project schedules.

If you have taken the time beforehand to do these projects yourself by all means use your experience to guide and assist students. Save sharing any actual artwork you created until after the students have completed the project as well. This gives the students the space to explore the materials and projects on their own.

Reflection...Express...
Explore...Empower...Expand...Freedom

SIX PROJECT CATEGORIES:

REFLECTION

These projects allow children to see themselves clearly in their art

1. I Am Here Flags - *pg. 132*
2. Animal Self-Portrait - *pg. 136*
3. Frida Mirror (handout) - *pg. 138*
4. Polka Dot Portrait - *pg. 144*
5. Courage Portrait (photo) - *pg. 164*
6. Symbol of Myself Mobile - *pg. 150*

EVERYONE IS AN ARTIST

EXPRESS

These projects allow children to define themselves.

1. Photo Self-Portrait - *pg. 140*
2. I Frame Myself (photo) - *pg. 166*
3. Tell a Tale Without Any Words - *pg. 174*
4. All of Me (photo) - *pg. 180*
5. Everyone Is an Artist Sign (handout) - *pg. 142*

RULE #1

EXPLORE

These projects help children search and find themselves in the world.

1. Map of Me - *pg. 156*
2. On My Block - *pg. 160*
3. Self-Portrait as Space - *pg. 170*

EMPOWER

These projects nurture confidence in the child's ability to create and encourage powerful reflections of one's self.

1. Making Face Puzzle (handout) - *pg. 130*
2. Emotions of Color - *pg. 148*
3. Boss of Me - *pg. 148*
4. Myself as Ancestor (photo) - *pg. 148*
5. There is Never a Right or Wrong Way to Make Art Sign (handout) - *pg. 152*

THERE IS NEVER A RIGHT OR WRONG WAY TO MAKE ART

RULE #2

EXPAND

These projects challenge children to explore beyond the norm.

1. Touch Your Face - *pg. 168*
2. What No One Can See - *pg. 172*
3. I Know the River Loves Me - *pg. 176*
4. Seeing Through Words (photo) - *pg. 178*

FREEDOM

These projects help children to shake free of limited thinking.

1. Wildest Self Collage - *pg. 134*
2. Cheat Please (photo) - *pg. 146*
3. Art Is Always an Act of Courage (handout) - *pg. 162*

ART IS ALWAYS AN ACT OF COURAGE

RULE #3

PROJECTS ORGANIZED BY ASSOCIATED BOOKS

This list organizes the projects by what books are used as a resource. Not all projects require books. The use of the book is not mandatory as the projects can stand on their own. If you can only buy one book, I recommend *Just Like Me: Stories and Self-Portraits by Fourteen Artists*. (Refer to *Chapter 4, Books: Behind the Story*, for more information about each of these books.)

My Colors, My World
1. Emotions of Color - *pg. 148*
2. Self-Portrait as Space or Place - *pg. 170*

I Know the River Loves Me
1. I Know the River Loves Me - *pg. 176*

Prietita and La Llorona
1. Animal Self-Portrait - *pg. 136*
2. Courage Portrait - *pg. 164*

Nana's Big Surprise
1. Symbol of Myself Mobile - *pg. 150*
2. Tell a Tale Without Words - *pg. 174*

My Diary From Here to There
1. Map of Me - *pg. 156*

My Very Own Room
1. Self-Portrait as Space or Place - *pg. 170*

Animal Poems of the Iquazu
1. Animal Self-Portrait - *pg. 136*
2, I Know the River Loves Me - *pg. 176*

Angels Ride Bikes and other Fall Poems
1. Making Face Puzzle- *pg. 130*
2. Cheat Please! - *pg. 146*

On My Block: Stories and Paintings by Fifteen Artists
1.On My Block - *pg. 160*

Honoring Our Ancestors: Stories and Portraits by Fourteen Artists
1. Myself as Ancestor - *pg. 158*

Just Like Me: Stories and Self-Portraits by Fourteen Artists
1. Photo Self-Portrait - *pg. 140*
2. What No One Can See Portrait - *pg. 172*
3. All of Me Portrait/Portrait/Portrait/Portrait - *pg. 180*
4. I Frame Myself-Word Window - *pg. 166*
5. Boss of Me Portrait - *pg. 154*
6. Wildest Self Collage - *pg. 134*

FUNDAMENTALS SCHEDULE:

This schedule allows for a monthly focus to integrate the curriculum in with other art or projects, if time is limited. Identify these projects by the fundamentals symbol in the top right corner.

1. Making Face Puzzle (handouts)/EMPOWER - *pg. 130*
2. Wildest Self Collage/FREEDOM - *pg. 134*
3. Everyone Is An Artist Sign (handout)EXPRESS - *pg. 142*
4. Emotions of Color/EMPOWER - *pg. 148*
5. Frida Mirror (handout)/REFLECTION** - *pg. 138*
6. There Is Never a Right or Wrong Way to Make Art Sign (handout)/EMPOWER - *pg. 152*
7. Art Is Always an Act of Courage Sign (handout)/FREEDOM - *pg. 162*
8. What No One Can See/EXPAND - *pg. 172*
9. Photo Self-Portrait/EXPRESS - *pg. 140*

CLAIMING FACE FULL SCHEDULE:

This schedule allows for deeper engagement through weekly art projects. The projects on the following pages follow the same order as this list.

** - indicates projects that offer specific opportunities for deeper study.

1. Making Face Puzzle (handout)/EMPOWER - *pg. 130*
2. I Am Here Flags/REFLECTION - *pg. 132*
3. Wildest Self Collage/FREEDOM - *pg. 134*
4. Animal Self-Portrait/REFLECTION** - *pg. 136*
5. Frida Mirror (handout)/REFLECTION** - *pg. 138*
6. Photo Self-Portrait (photo)/EXPRESS - *pg. 140*
7. Everyone Is an Artist Sign (handout)/EXPRESS - *pg. 142*
8. Polka Dot Portrait/REFLECTION - *pg. 144*
9. Cheat Please! (photo)/FREEDOM - *pg. 146*
10. Emotions of Color/EMPOWER - *pg. 148*
11. Symbol of Myself Mobile/REFLECTION - *pg. 150*
12. There is Never a Right or Wrong Way to Make Art Sign (handout)/EMPOWER - *pg. 152*
13. Boss of Me Portrait/EMPOWER - *pg. 154*
14. Map of Me/EXPLORE** - *pg. 156*
15. Myself as Ancestor (photo)/EMPOWER - *pg. 158*
16. On My Block/EXPLORE** - *pg. 160*
17. Art Is Always an Act of Courage (handout)/FREEDOM - *pg. 162*
18. Courage Portrait (photo)/REFLECTION - *pg. 164*
19. I Frame Myself-Word Window (photo)/EXPRESS - *pg. 166*
20. Touch Your Face/EXPAND - *pg. 168*
21. Self-Portrait as Space or Place/EXPLORE - *pg. 170*
22. What No One Can See/EXPAND - *pg. 172*
23. Tell a Tale Without Words/EXPRESS - *pg. 174*
24. I Know the River Loves Me (photo)/EXPAND** - *pg. 176*
25. Seeing Through Words (photo)/EXPAND - *pg. 178*
26. All of Me Portrait/Portrait/Portrait/Portrait (photo)/EXPRESS - *pg. 180*

an image created of one's self with the purpose of expressing experience, claiming self, creating reflection and knowing one's self more deeply.

SELF-PORTRAIT (n.)

"a people should not long for their own image."

CLAIMING FACE
Self-Empowerment through Self-Portraiture

26 Projects

Making Face Step-by-Step

Fig. 1

Fig. 2

Fig. 3

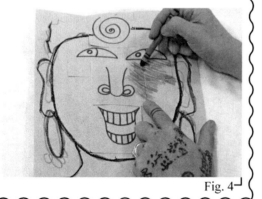

Fig. 4

Classroom Notes:

What I learned from doing the project myself:

What did or didn't work in the classroom:

How I would change or modify the project:

Inspirations, new ideas & directions, other projects:

1.Making Face
Puzzle

FUNDAMENTALS #1   EMPOWER

Purpose of Project:

This project is a great ice breaker. It is **enjoyable** and meant to be **funny**. Art is play. Based primarily on making choices and putting things together, this project begins building confidence by engaging with familiar materials. It introduces the concept of using the face as a place of expression.

Process:

1. Have one pile of the mouths, eyes, ears, noses and wild squares in the center for each table or group of artists.

2. Direct each artist to discover and choose 7 elements.

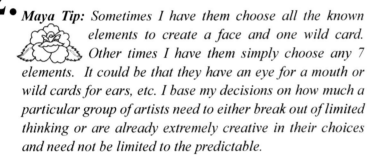

Maya Tip: Sometimes I have them choose all the known elements to create a face and one wild card. Other times I have them simply choose any 7 elements. It could be that they have an eye for a mouth or wild cards for ears, etc. I base my decisions on how much a particular group of artists need to either break out of limited thinking or are already extremely creative in their choices and need not be limited to the predictable.

GUIDE ARTISTS IN THE FOLLOWING STEPS:

3. On blank sheet, glue all elements into place except ears and wild card. Make sure the edges of the squares are glued down flat. *(Fig. 2)*

4. Draw a head shape to contain facial elements which may entail drawing over parts of the squares (this is why it is important to glue down all edges). *(Fig. 3)*

5. Glue or draw on ears and place wild element where desired.

6. With crayons color entire piece as much as possible, try to ignore the edges of the glued down pieces. Add hair. Add neck and shoulders. Or horns, fins, tails! Remember the art in **Angles Ride Bikes**? Cover all of the pieces and the background with color to create a complete image. *(Fig. 4)*

7. Sign your work.

PREP

- Copy Making Face Handouts on a creme or white cardstock *(15 copies of each handout for class size of 30)*
- Cut into squares (ie. one mouth per square) and divide into even piles for each group of artists. *(Fig. 1)*

MATERIALS

- Making Face Handouts *(pg. 212-213)*
- Scissors (only for your prep)
- Glue sticks (definitely not wet glue)
- Crayons
- Pencils
- One blank sheet of paper per artwork

BOOKS

Angels Ride Bikes and Other Summer Poems by Francisco Alarcon
How I made the art in this book is essentially what they will be doing for this project.

I AM HERE
Step-by-Step

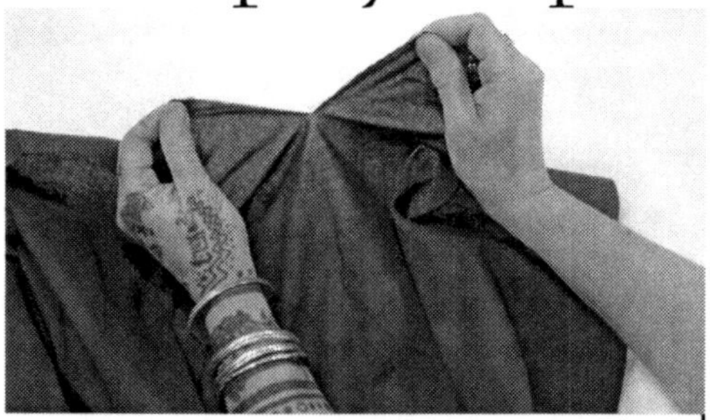

Fig. 1

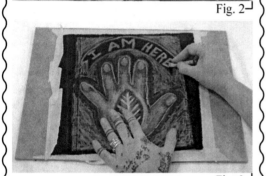

Fig. 2

Fig. 3

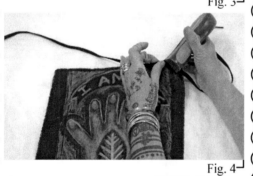

Fig. 4

Fig. 5

Classroom Notes:

What I learned from doing the project myself:

What did or didn't work in the classroom:

How I would change or modify the project:

Inspirations, new ideas & directions, other projects:

2.I AM HERE
Flags/Hand Portraits

REFLECTION

Purpose of Project:

Hands are one of the oldest and immediate forms of artistic expression that says "I am here." Creating and displaying these pieces is a **beautiful** and **powerful** statement of presence for our artists to see every day in the classroom or outside the window. They are simple to create and absolutely stunning. Visual beauty is vital to see in our world and ourselves. It is a reflection of our inner being. By stating clearly that "I am here" it promotes that each artist belongs here and is seen.

Process:

1. Tape all the way around edge of the cloth onto desk or board to make it the most secure. It is easier to draw with pastels if the cloth is stabilized.

GUIDE ARTISTS IN THE FOLLOWING STEPS:

2. Place hand in center of square and trace closely around it with oil pastel. *(Fig. 2)*

3. Decorate your hand portrait as desired. Use favorite colors, decorations, and images of things you love.

4. When portrait is complete, draw a border and write "I am here" and your name. *(Fig. 3)*

5. Remove tape.

6. Staple the tops of the cloth squares along the ribbon like flags hanging down. *(Fig. 4)*

7. Hang in classroom or outside of a window in view of classroom. This can be done as a class or solely by the educator.

 Teacher Tips: Pastels can get on desks if project is taped to desk. It cleans off, but to avoid more work use an Art Board or piece of cardboard for a work space. Refer to Ch. 7, pg. 98 for more about Art Boards.
Rip the cloth instead of cutting as this often ensures a straight line. Measure the 9x9 grid and make a small cut with scissors at the top then grab either side of cut and rip cloth, shown in Fig. 1.

PREP

- Purchase 2 yards of black cloth
- Measure out a 9x9 grid
- Cut/rip cloth into 32-9x9 squares *(Fig. 1)*
- 30 -10 x 12 Art boards to tape cloth down to (if you choose)

MATERIALS

- Black cotton cloth, ripped or cut into approx. 9x9 inch squares, (at least one per artist)
- Scissors (only for your prep)
- Heavy cotton ribbon
- Stapler & Staples
- Masking tape
- Desk top or art board (per artist)
- Oil pastels

BOOKS

No specific book for this project.
Recommend downloading images from the internet to show students:

Pre-historic hands painted on rocks and in caves.

Wildest Self
Step-by-Step

Fig. 1

Fig. 2

Fig. 3

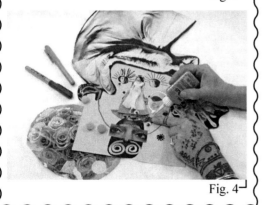

Fig. 4

Classroom Notes:

What I learned from doing the project myself:

What did or didn't work in the classroom:

How I would change or modify the project:

Inspirations, new ideas & directions, other projects:

3. Wildest Self
Collage

FUNDAMENTALS #2   FREEDOM

Purpose of Project:

This project is meant to expand perception of self and support open, creative, fearless expression of self. This supports **dismantling judgment** of a right or wrong way. Like in *Chapter 3, Rebel!*, pg 37, this gives the artist "formal" permission to be as expressive as possible. Wild! Kids sometimes feel like they're being very "edge-y" or even "bad" with how wild they can make their piece. It's as if they're breaking real rules! Sometimes they'll ask, but can I do THIS? What about THIS? And I always say you can do no wrong. *"I am not afraid of your art. Do whatever you need to do."*

Process:

1. Distribute magazines evenly for each group of artists and instruct them to cut out or gather images that interest them from the magazines. Advise not to think too many thoughts, like *"I need two eyes"* or *"I have to have hands."* Encourage them to just gather. *(Fig. 1)*

GUIDE ARTISTS IN THE FOLLOWING STEPS:

2. When you feel like you have a good pile of images or even just pieces of images, lay them out on your workspace. Swirl them around, pick pieces up and place in different places. *(Fig. 2)* See if any images are drawn to other images or in different patterns. Pretend to "listen" to the images and do what they say. Maybe you collected all mouths and your entire face is made of mouths. Maybe you have 20 arms or are floating with a cloud as a body.

Maya Tip: I'm often surprised by this one. Stories and shapes will rise that I never would have expected because I'm choosing from a wide range of images instead of what I like to draw.

3. Begin gluing the images onto their base piece of paper in relation to the "story" you heard them tell you. Or, you could simply begin gluing down the pieces and let the process unfold as you go. Sometimes it is fun to see what happens without any plan at all. *(Fig. 3)*

4. Layer optional items and/or draw on top of the main image. It adds a whole other dimension and can create a unifying effect. *(Fig. 4)*

5. Title and sign your work. For example, *"I am a Giant Squid with Lipstick"* by Maya.

PREP

• Collect various magazines

MATERIALS

• Magazines of ALL kinds
• Scissors
• Glue sticks
• One blank sheet of paper per artwork

Optional:

• Glitter glue, Wiggle eyes, Puff balls, Yarn, Beads, sequins, etc.

BOOKS

Just Like Me: Fourteen Stories and Self-Portraits by Fourteen Artists
Specifically, Rudolfo Morales' piece. He identifies which character is him.
Picasso or Chagall art books
These artists have images that challenge what a face should look like. Chagall's work will show a face, but the head will be upside down or brilliant green. In one self-portrait he has seven fingers. Why does he have seven fingers? What could he be trying to tell us?

Animal Self Step-by-Step

Classroom Notes:

What I learned from doing the project myself:

Fig. 1

What did or didn't work in the classroom:

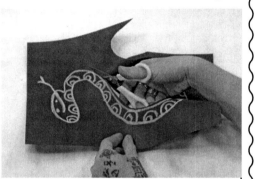

Fig. 2

How I would change or modify the project:

Fig. 3

Inspirations, new ideas & directions, other projects:

Fig. 4

4. Animal Self-Portrait

REFLECTION

Purpose of Project:

There are aspects of our selves that are sometimes best felt and expressed through an animal counterpart. Some animals are feral. They are outside of human context. Some are deeply associated with home, like domestic friends. Some are weak and vulnerable, others are massively powerful. Associating an aspect of our self as an animal frees us up to see and experience more of ourselves. It also provides us with the opportunity to call in qualities we might not have. Beyond this it personalizes animals. Once you know you're part bear you will have an inner feeling for bears and the environment where they live, creating a more environmentally conscious person on our planet. It also supports the sense that nature is a part of us and we belong here as naturally as a bear in the woods.

 PREP

- This project offers **opportunity for greater study**.
- Have students choose and research an animal to be in their self-portrait.
- Research includes: appearance, habitat, food, strengths, habits, everything!

 MATERIALS

- Drawing or painting materials. Either use all crayons or all colored pencils or all watercolors
- Scissors
- Color Construction paper
- Glue sticks
- Crayons
- Pencils
- One blank sheet of paper per artwork

Process:

GUIDE ARTISTS IN THE FOLLOWING STEPS:

1. Using one medium, either drawing or painting, create a portrait of your animal. *(Fig. 1)*

2. Once finished painting or drawing, cut your animal out. *(Fig. 2)*

3. Using the color construction paper cut out pieces to create your animal's world: leaves, flowers, mountains, sky, water. *(Fig. 3)*

4. Glue down all the pieces with your animal deep in the environment that you created. *(Fig. 4)*

5. Sign your work.

 BOOKS

Animal Poems of the Iguazu
by Francisco Alarcon

Prietita and the Ghost Woman
by Gloria Anzuldua

Frida Mirror
Step-by-Step

Fig. 1

Fig. 2

Classroom Notes:

What I learned from doing the project myself:

What did or didn't work in the classroom:

How I would change or modify the project:

Inspirations, new ideas & directions, other projects:

5.Frida Mirror

Purpose of Project:

This project uses another artist as a way to begin expressing potentially **deeper emotions** and a more **complicated sense of self**. Frida Kahlo almost exclusively used self-portraiture as a tool to affirm her existence and navigate her deepest feelings. She is also a widely visible artist today, especially in Mexican culture. Her images are quite literally everywhere in the US and Mexico, making her a familiar icon. She can serve as a model in both how she used art and that she is celebrated for it.

Process:

1. Distribute Frida handout to each artist.

GUIDE ARTISTS IN THE FOLLOWING STEPS:

2. Imagine that the image of Frida is actually your mirror in the morning when you get up to brush your teeth. See her face as your own face. Look closely at all the details. The tears, the bird, the shape of her mouth. What is she telling us with this drawing, especially with the bird? How do you imagine she feels? Have you ever felt this way? How are you feeling now? *(Fig. 1)*

3. Use oil pastels to color over her face, show what you feel. *(Fig. 2)*

> ***Maya Tip:*** *Some of the Frida's I have seen: it could be that the tears are accentuated or colored over completely. She could have angry horns or a huge smile. She may be a painted clown or wearing a wrestling mask. She may be a skeleton or a ghost. She may be a shy cat. She may be in flames or covered in words or look like a tiny baby.*

4. Sign your work.

PREP

- This project offers **opportunity for greater study**.
- With your class, study Frida Kahlo's art and how art served her, her life, her country, her husband, Diego Rivera.
- Copy Frida handout at least one per artist

MATERIALS

- Frida Handout *(pg. 214)*
- Oil Pastels

BOOKS

Any of Frida Kahlo's books showing her art are appropriate.

Please share what you are most comfortable answering questions about, since some of her images are strong. The image I use here is from *Frida Kahlo The Brush of Anguish* by Martha Zamora, page 85.

Also *Frida* by Scholastic Press is a beautiful children's book.

Photo Self-Portrait Step-by-Step

Fig. 1

Fig. 2

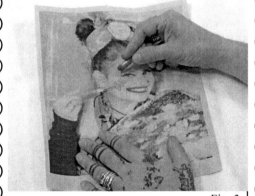

Fig. 3

Classroom Notes:

What I learned from doing the project myself:

What did or didn't work in the classroom:

How I would change or modify the project:

Inspirations, new ideas & directions, other projects:

6.Photo Self-Portrait

FUNDAMENTALS #9   EXPRESS

Purpose of Project:

I just have to say that this project is **gorgeous.** While I think it is valuable to do the project for reasons I will explain. There is **great power** in creating something that is simply beautiful *AND* I think there is something special about creating something beautiful that looks just like you. Beyond that, spending time looking into your own face is a good meditation to see and **know more and more of yourself.**

This project builds on the project, *The Frida Mirror,* allowing your **own face to be your home,** your place of art, your place to express something that occurred that day, that week. I've seen some kids color their selves as close to "real" life as possible, while others have flowers growing across their forehead or giant tears. Sometimes the only comment they have about the giant tears are that they are decoration. Never draw too much attention to what an artist is creating while they are creating. Let them come to full completion. Always make open, "seeing" statements through the process. *"I see these big blue shapes around your eyes on your face. The blue is darker around the edges. I notice you have 4 of these shapes so far."* If you feel compelled to ask questions, hold them until after the artist has let go of the piece. Then the two of you can look at it together and the artist can take you on a tour of their portrait. Ask if it is okay to ask questions? Admit that you are very curious about their piece.

 PREP

- Photograph students (see *Working with Photographs* in *Chapter 7,* pages 96-97).
- Print/copy one "regular" and one "wild" image per student on heavy cardstock paper. *(Fig. 1)*

 MATERIALS

- "Regular" and "Wild" Photo of each student, printed on cardstock
- Oil pastels

 BOOKS

Just Like Me: Stories and Self-portraits by Fourteen Artists
This is a great book to show different ways to portray one's self. I love all of them! Look at Rodolfo Morales' collage. Look how Stephen Von Mason and Joesam paint themselves! Joesam's shirt even says artist on it. And how about Michele Wood? And Mira has her whole family and her cats!

Process:

1. Distribute photos to each artist.

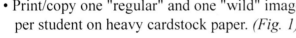 *Maya Tip: I rarely say much with this project other than, "Color your image exactly how you need to today."*

GUIDE ARTISTS IN THE FOLLOWING STEPS:

2. Use oil pastels to color and decorate directly over the photo image. *(Fig. 2 & 3)*

3. Sign your work.

Everyone is an Artist
Step-by-Step

Fig. 1

Fig. 2

Fig. 3

Classroom Notes:

What I learned from doing the project myself:

What did or didn't work in the classroom:

How I would change or modify the project:

Inspirations, new ideas & directions, other projects:

7. "Everyone is an Artist" Sign

FUNDAMENTALS #3 EXPRESS

Purpose of Project:

My terribly important **Rules** are covered in *Chapter 6, The 3 Rules*. We take the time to create our own sign for each rule in order to **claim them personally** as our own and to allow the information to enter us through different modalities. It also gives us the excuse to color it and decorate it, affect it with our own flavor! All part of the claiming process. Literally make it our own. In the *Imagine* exercise for *Chapter 6 (pg. 78)* you embodied and then drew **The Rules**. Practicing drawing the symbol of **the 3 Rules** while you explain the different parts would be one way that as a class you all learn as much as you can about **The Rules**.

Process:

1. Distribute signs and blank paper to each artist.

Guide Artists in the Following Steps:

2. Decorate and color your sign. *(Fig. 2)*

3. Using the blank paper, make another sign of your own that reads: *(Fig. 3)*
 "I AM AN ARTIST"

4. Sign your work.

5. When all artwork is complete, ask each artist to stand up, hold up one of their signs and read it out loud to the class.

PREP

• Copy *Everyone Is an Artist* handout at least one sign per student. *(Fig. 1)*

MATERIALS

• *Everyone Is an Artist/Rule #1* handout; *(pg. 215)*

• One blank sheet of paper per artwork

• Something to mark with: crayons, pencils, markers, pastels, paints…

BOOKS

The students can claim any book they want for this one. This encourages them to connect with a book for themselves and possibly see themselves in the story, the author or the artist. I like Dr. Suess an awful lot. I fancy I might choose one of his.

Polka Dot
Step-by-Step

Fig. 1

Fig. 2

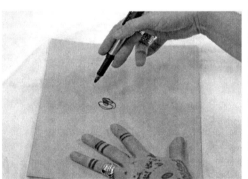

Fig. 3

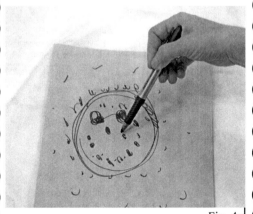

Fig. 4

Classroom Notes:

What I learned from doing the project myself:

What did or didn't work in the classroom:

How I would change or modify the project:

Inspirations, new ideas & directions, other projects:

8.Polka Dot Portrait

Purpose of Project:

My *Polka Dot Theory* is covered in *Chapter 6, The 3 Rules*. I have witnessed much art making in my work and what I have noticed is that no one marks the page in the same way. Literally, our very bodies carry our uniqueness. If I make a polka dot on the page and you make one and another person makes one, we can tell who made which polka dot. How we carry our stories and experiences affects how we hold our hand, touch a pencil, apply pressure and execute something as basic as a dot. Just a dot shows something that is all our own. My polka dot is mine and only mine. And yours can only be yours. This is the beginning of art. This project gives us the opportunity to notice what is **uniquely our own**.

Process:

1. If you have *The Dot* book feel free to explore with your class the many dots that are possible. You simply cannot go wrong with a dot. Dots rock!

GUIDE ARTISTS IN THE FOLLOWING STEPS:

2. Dot it! Do one, do two, do three, do four. MAKE YOUR MARK! *(Fig. 2, 3, & 4)*

3. One dot on one page. Ten dots on another. What ever feels good. What are all the ways to make a dot? Look closely at your dots. Are they big, small, swirly, dark, or..?

4. Sign your work.

MATERIALS

• Something to mark paper: pencils, crayons, pastels, watercolors, you name it!

• **Lots** of blank paper

BOOKS

The Dot by Peter Reynolds
I was thrilled to discover this book. Apparently he knows the truth about polka dots too! Truth is truth. It belongs to all of us and it is good to pass it around as much as possible! This is a great book to have in the classroom. I highly recommend it. Scholastic and Fablevision have also made this book into an animated short film.

Cheat Please!
Step-by-Step

Fig. 1

Fig. 2

Fig. 3

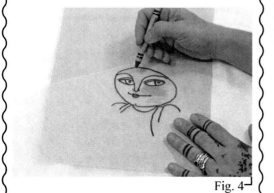

Fig. 4

Classroom Notes:

What I learned from doing the project myself:

What did or didn't work in the classroom:

How I would change or modify the project:

Inspirations, new ideas & directions, other projects:

9.Cheat Please!

FREEDOM

Purpose of Project:

In *Behind the Story* in *Chapter 8*, I talk about how the art came about for the book, *Angels Ride Bikes and Other Summer Poems*. I have read studies that echo what I've been saying for years. Something changes in relation to creativity about 4th grade. We can affect this by **freeing up some of the judgment and limitation** that becomes a challenge from this age on. Here we allow our students to cross the line with permission like in *Rebel!*, *Chapter 3, pg. 37*. Built upon the prior projects, like the *Polka Dot Portrait*, they may now understand that just their hand carries something wholly their own. Even as they trace an image, they are showing themselves.

Process:

1. Take a poll in your class of who believes you can cheat when you make art. Afterwards, explore what "cheating" means and how exactly would you cheat making art. Then bring up the *Polka Dot Theory*. If just making a polka dot shows something about who you are, what could tracing an entire picture show you about yourself. Look at *Angels Ride Bikes* and see if your students can locate the "cheat" lines.

Guide Artists in the Following Steps:

2. Using tracing paper, trace your image or book image in pencil or pen. *(Fig. 2 & 3)*

3. Remove traced image from book and color with crayons or oil pastels. *(Fig. 4)*

4. Sign your work.

PREP

• Have students choose a book of either a favorite story, a favorite artist, or a photo of themselves. *(Fig. 1)*

MATERIALS

• Image to trace, either self-portraits or scene from favorite book
• Tracing Paper
• Pencils or Markers
• Crayons or Oil Pastels

BOOKS

Angels Ride Bikes and Other Summer Poems by Francisco Alarcon.
I tried to cheat as much as possible in this book!

Emotions of Color
Step-by-Step

Fig. 1

Fig. 2

Fig. 3

Classroom Notes:

What I learned from doing the project myself:

What did or didn't work in the classroom:

How I would change or modify the project:

Inspirations, new ideas & directions, other projects:

10. Emotions of Color

FUNDAMENTALS #4   EMPOWER

Purpose of Project:

Does a painting that is all red feel different than a painting that is all blue? What colors feel happy, mad, sad, scared, peaceful, confused? Any of them? Sometimes we all agree how a color feels. Sometimes there are colors that only feel that way to one of us and no one else. Red is a great one to explore. I turn my back to the students and scrunch up my face and try to get myself to actually turn red, then turn around with a bit of a grimace and ask the kids what color I am and how do they imagine I feel. They usually say mad. Sometimes they even tell stories about someone they know who was that mad and turned red. Then I **explore** other reds with them. Red for love, like for Valentine's Day. Red is the color of blood and could represent life and birth! Fire is red too! Fire is hot. Is red hot? What color makes them feel peaceful? What color is happy? **This adds a dimension** to the tools available to express more and more.

Process:

1. Ask some questions to get started:
Do you have a favorite color? Why that one or two or ? Do you see it now? How do you feel when you see it? Does it remind you of yourself? What if your whole world turned beige, what's the first color you'd want to see?

GUIDE ARTISTS IN THE FOLLOWING STEPS:

2. Do a drawing of yourself completely in your favorite color. *(Fig. 1)*

3. Include anything else that reminds you of that color. *(Fig. 2)*

> *Maya Tip:* for example, I would do a drawing of myself totally in hot pink with the hot pink sunset in a heart.

4. Name the color distinctly.

> *Maya Tip:* for example, mine is HOT pink. Yellow could be lemon or golden or sunshine or fire-y.

5. Write color name and sign. *(Fig. 3)*

MATERIALS

- Oil pastels or crayons or colored pencils or whatever marks color on paper
- One blank sheet of paper per artwork

BOOKS

My Colors, My World
by Maya Gonzalez
In this story the colors are all covered up by a wind storm. The girl discovers herself and her world as she begins to see color.

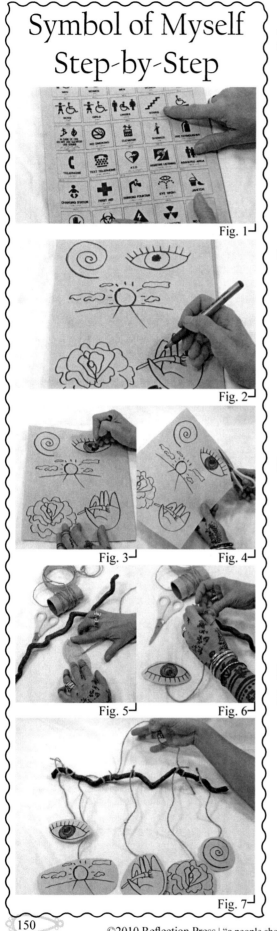

Symbol of Myself Step-by-Step

Fig. 1

Fig. 2

Fig. 3   Fig. 4

Fig. 5   Fig. 6

Fig. 7

Classroom Notes:

What I learned from doing the project myself:

What did or didn't work in the classroom:

How I would change or modify the project:

Inspirations, new ideas & directions, other projects:

11. Symbol of Myself
Mobile
 REFLECTION

Purpose of Project:

We often have something that we ALWAYS draw or even doodle. Sometimes it shows something as simple as how our hand likes to move. Sometimes there's a particular image we often find ourselves drawing. I draw eyes a lot. When I think about it, seeing, being seen, and perceiving things have been key lessons in my life. So to symbolize myself, I might draw an eye. Or, I might draw a Hot Pink Swirl to symbolize the sunset where I found my reflection as a child in *My Colors, My World*. These very small images feel like me. This project allows us to **distill ourselves**. It shows us the most basic, fundamental aspect of our self.

Process:

1. Explore the concept of symbols by looking at those in the classroom or imagining those in everyday life. Symbols are like small pictures to tell you something quickly. Like a stop sign or the little white figure on a walk sign. *(Fig. 1)*

GUIDE ARTISTS IN THE FOLLOWING STEPS:

2. Draw 5 (or more) very simple images that symbolize something about you. Is it a shape, an animal, a tree, a favorite hat, initials, key, heart? *(Fig. 2)*

3. Color each of your symbols. *(Fig. 3)*

4. Cut out each of your symbols. *(Fig. 4)*

5. Tape each of your symbols onto string or twine and tie the string onto your stick in any arrangement you want. *(Fig. 5&6)*

6. Tie an additional piece of string or twine onto the top of your symbol mobile to hang. *(Fig. 7)*

7. Sign your work - this could be done on the back of one of your symbols or your name could be attached as a symbol itself.

8. Hang mobiles in your classroom. Can you tell which mobile belongs to who without looking at their name?

 Teacher Tip: You could even explore the symbols related to the CLAIMING FACE curriculum with your class.

 PREP

- Go on a walk in nature or around your school exploring symbols.
- Have students gather sticks during the walk, or provide sticks.

 **MATERIALS**

- Markers or oil pastels
- Two blank sheets of paper per mobile
- Twine, String or Yarn
- Scissors
- Tape
- Stick

 **BOOKS**

Nana's Big Surprise
　　　　by Amada Irma Perez
The keys, heart milagros and the shawl are all symbols. The keys symbolize the children's relationship with their grandmother. How the heart milagros and the shawl change symbolize the change in the grandmothers emotions.

Never Right or Wrong
Step-by-Step

Fig. 1

Fig. 2

Classroom Notes:

What I learned from doing the project myself:

What did or didn't work in the classroom:

How I would change or modify the project:

Inspirations, new ideas & directions, other projects:

12. "There is Never a Right or Wrong Way to Make Art" Sign

FUNDAMENTALS #6   EMPOWER

Purpose of Project:

My terribly important **RULES** are covered in *Chapter 6, The 3 Rules*. We take the time to create our own sign for each to claim them personally as our own and to allow the information to enter us through different modalities. It also gives us the excuse to color it and decorate it, affect it with our own flavor! All part of the **claiming process**. Literally make it our own. **This one is vital for 4th grade and up.** In the *Imagine* exercise for *Chapter 6 (pg. 78)* you embodied and then drew **THE RULES**. Practicing drawing the symbol of **THE 3 RULES** while you explain the different parts would be one way that as a class you all learn as much as you can about **THE RULES**.

Process:

1. Distribute sign to each artist.

GUIDE ARTISTS IN THE FOLLOWING STEPS:

2. Decorate and color your sign. *(Fig. 2)*

3. Sign your work.

4. When all artwork is complete, have each artist stand up, hold up their sign and read it out loud to the class.

PREP

• Copy *There is Never a Right or Wrong Way to Make Art* handout at least one sign per artist. *(Fig. 1)*

MATERIALS

• *There is Never a Right or Wrong Way to Make Art/Rule #2* handout; *(pg. 216)*

• Something to mark with: crayons, pencils, markers, pastels, paints…

BOOKS

Picasso Art books
What if Picasso had thought "oh no, I can't possibly do this. It's all wrong." The world would be a different place without Picasso's amazing, mind and eyeball-stretching art. We need everyone's vision to make this a world for all of us to not only be, but also learn from each other.

Boss of Me
Step-by-Step

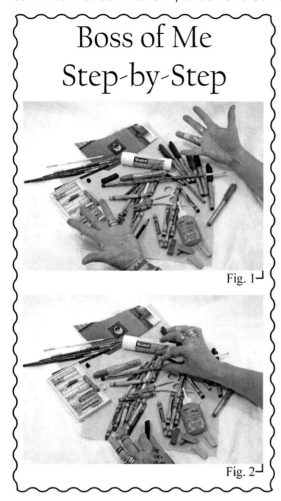

Fig. 1⌐

Fig. 2⌐

Classroom Notes:

What I learned from doing the project myself:

What did or didn't work in the classroom:

How I would change or modify the project:

Inspirations, new ideas & directions, other projects:

13. Boss of Me
Portrait

EMPOWER

Purpose of Project:

This project formally grounds the **2ND RULE** and its accompanying theory, *Boss of Me.* **Experience supports knowing.** Only we can truly know ourselves. Here we exercise that by choosing our materials and what we're going to create.

Process:

Maya Tip: *It is generous for you as the educator to take the time to provide as many options as possible for your students for this project. There may be no "thank you" coming your way, but it's important for children to know that they have choices in their lives. Even these small choices can make a difference. I thank you for your great patience and commitment. Your work is very important.*

GUIDE ARTISTS IN THE FOLLOWING STEPS:

1. Do what you must. This is your moment to use what materials call you and create any kind of art, self-portrait or not that you feel you must create to show everyone that you are the boss of you. No one else can know you, no one else can be you, no one else can show us what you can.

2. Sign your work.

3. When all artwork is complete, have each artist share and thank them for completing this project.

PREP

• It may take some preparation to accommodate this project, but it is very important to do. Give yourself the time necessary to make this happen as smoothly as possible.

• Determine all of the available art materials in your classroom and if possible include an unknown material like charcoal or watercolor pencils

• It may be helpful to poll your students ahead of time to see what materials they want to work with

• Organize how to manage diverse materials being used simultaneously, one idea is to have specific stations for each separate material

MATERIALS

• Entirely up to the student.

BOOKS

Just Like Me: Stories and Self-Portraits by Fourteen Artists
Each of these artists is demonstrating their individuality and self expression in the colors they choose, the styles they work in, the stories they choose to share.

Map of Me
Step-by-Step

Fig. 1

Fig. 2

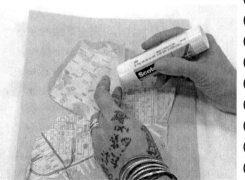

Fig. 3

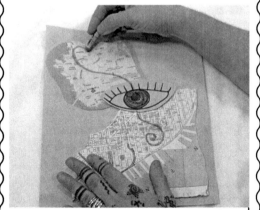

Fig. 4

Classroom Notes:

What I learned from doing the project myself:

What did or didn't work in the classroom:

How I would change or modify the project:

Inspirations, new ideas & directions, other projects:

14.Map of Me

EXPLORE

Purpose of Project:

There are big maps and small maps. This is a big map project. (*On My Block is the small map project*) Because of how this country developed, most all of us come from somewhere else. Although some of us have been here so long, we think only of this country. Many of us still feel connected to another country or have family in another country. This project allows us to use art to explore our sense of place and make **unifying connections** that **Earth is home**. Maps are art.

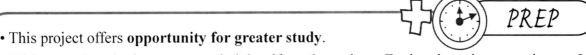 *PREP*

- This project offers **opportunity for greater study**.
- With your class, look at maps, and globes if you have them. Explore how these are also art. Look for all the signs that these are pieces of art. Make as many connections on the map as possible. What proximity is the town where you live in relation to the town where you were born. *(Fig. 1)*
- Poll your students ahead of time to see what countries they want to include. Could be countries where they feel any connection or the places where they've traveled.
- Collect and copy enough of all necessary maps.

Process:

GUIDE ARTISTS IN THE FOLLOWING STEPS:

1. Layer pieces of the maps that relate to you on your base piece of paper, play with the arrangement. Are some places far away physically, but feel very close in your heart? Move the maps around so that they convey something about how you feel about them. *(Fig. 2)*
Maya Tip: *I like to tear the edges, but you could cut them of course.*

2. Glue the maps onto the paper in the arrangement desired. *(Fig. 3)*

3. Using the oil pastels create paths between the places on the maps. You can use colors to represent what's important. Or use your Symbol to show where you are on the map, either in body or in thoughts. This could be made on another piece of paper, cut out, and placed in the piece. *(Fig. 4)*

4. Decorate. Glitter if desired!

5. Sign your work.

 *MATERIALS*

- Maps
- Oil Pastels
- Scissors
- One blank sheet of paper per artwork

Optional:
- Glitter or Glitter Glue

 *BOOKS*

My Diary from Here to There
by Amada Irma Perez
Based on the story in this book, I imagine if little Amada was doing this project she would include maps of both Mexico and the United States.

Myself as Ancestor
Step-by-Step

Fig. 1

Fig. 2

Classroom Notes:

What I learned from doing the project myself:

What did or didn't work in the classroom:

How I would change or modify the project:

Inspirations, new ideas & directions, other projects:

15. Myself as Ancestor

EMPOWER

Purpose of Project:

It's interesting to imagine what you might be like when you are old. It shows us what is important to us right now and extends an imaginative path to fulfilling it. It also connects us to our elders in our community and connects us with the older person we will be, perhaps inspiring a sense of **wisdom and endurance**. Great Grandma Maya. I can totally see myself!

Process:

GUIDE ARTISTS IN THE FOLLOWING STEPS:

1. Imagine yourself very old. You are an ancestor. Can you see yourself? What have you been up to? What does your life look like? What was the most important thing to you?

> **Maya Tip:** *I love to imagine myself as old. Some of the things I like to think about are how much art I will have made, how many kids I will have gotten to play with, and how I'll probably dress even wilder the older I am.*

2. Now color yourself, but adding the different things that might have changed as you've been alive a really long time. Lines? Gray hair? Different hairdo? Add anything in the picture that tells us what kind of life you've lived. *(Fig. 2)*

3. Sign your work.

PREP

- Photograph students (see *Working with Photographs* in *Chapter 7*, pages 96-97).
- Print/copy one "regular" photo per student on heavy cream colored cardstock.

MATERIALS

- "Regular" photo of each student printed on cardstock
- Oil Pastels

BOOKS

Honoring Our Ancestors: Stories and Portraits by Fourteen Artists
In this book different artists look at the ancestors that inspired them.

On My Block
Step-by-Step

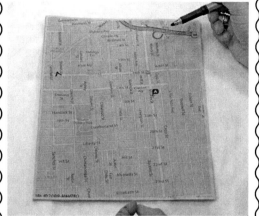

Fig. 1

Fig. 2

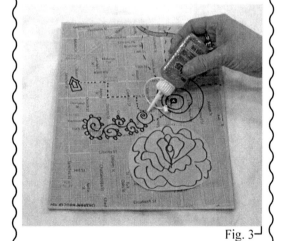

Fig. 3

Classroom Notes:

What I learned from doing the project myself:

What did or didn't work in the classroom:

How I would change or modify the project:

Inspirations, new ideas & directions, other projects:

16.On My Block

EXPLORE

Purpose of Project:

This is the small map project, related to *Map of Myself.* Here we look at our more intimate path in life. Home, neighborhood, school. Study where you live, and make a map of your daily life. This contributes to **being present in the here and now.** What do you see? What is the shape of your path?

Process:

1. Distribute copy of map to each artist.

GUIDE ARTISTS IN THE FOLLOWING STEPS:

2. Study the map of your town or city and locate where your important places are. *(Fig. 1)*

3. Mark the paths you follow between the important places in your life on your map. *(Fig. 2)*

4. Draw pictures or symbols of the places that are important to you in your town. Home? School? Parks? Special centers? Your auntie's store? Your mother's job?

5. If desired, you can draw pictures or symbols on another sheet of paper, cut out, and place anywhere on your map. *(Fig. 3)*

6. Decorate as necessary, add glitter if desired. *(Fig. 3)*

7. Sign your work.

PREP

- This project offers **opportunity for greater study.**
- With your class, study about the town or region where you live.
- Make copies of a map of your town, neighborhood or region (at least one copy per artist). *(Fig. 1)*

MATERIALS

- Map of town or region for each student.
- Oil Pastels or Color Pencils or Markers

Optional:
- Glitter or Glitter Glue, glue stick
- Additional paper and scissors for making symbol or pictures

BOOKS

On My Block: Stories and Paintings by Fifteen Artists
Neighborhoods are very important. It's where our home is, where we live, where we spend our time.

Act of Courage Step-by-Step

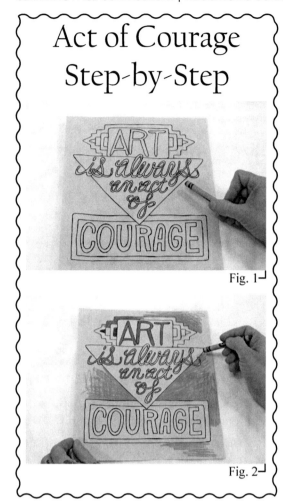

Fig. 1

Fig. 2

Classroom Notes:

What I learned from doing the project myself:

What did or didn't work in the classroom:

How I would change or modify the project:

Inspirations, new ideas & directions, other projects:

17. "Art is Always an Act of Courage" Sign

FUNDAMENTALS #7   FREEDOM

Purpose of Project:

My terribly important **RULES** are covered in *Chapter 6, The 3 Rules*. We take the time to create our own sign for each to claim them personally as our own and to allow the information to enter us through different modalities. It also gives us the excuse to color it and decorate it, affect it with our own flavor! All part of **the claiming process**. Literally make it our own. **This one is as important as the 2nd rule for 4th grade and up.** In the *Imagine* exercise for *Chapter 6 (pg. 78)* you embodied and then drew THE RULES. Practicing drawing the symbol of THE 3 RULES while you explain the different parts would be one way that as a class you all learn as much as you can about THE RULES.

Process:

1. Distribute sign to each artist.

GUIDE ARTISTS IN THE FOLLOWING STEPS:

1. Decorate and color your sign. *(Fig. 2)*

2. Pay attention to the courage you feel rising inside of you while you flavor this sign with your own markings!

3. Sign your work.

4. When all artwork is complete, have each artist stand up, hold up their sign and read it out loud to the class.

PREP

• Copy *Art is Always an Act of Courage* handout at least one sign per student. *(Fig. 1)*

MATERIALS

• *Art is Always an Act of Courage/ Rule #3* handout; *(pg. 217)*

• Something to mark with: crayons, pencils, markers, pastels, paints…

BOOKS

Any book!
If there's art in it, there is courage in it even if the story doesn't speak about it.

Courage
Step-by-Step

Fig. 1

Fig. 2

Fig. 3

Classroom Notes:

What I learned from doing the project myself:

What did or didn't work in the classroom:

How I would change or modify the project:

Inspirations, new ideas & directions, other projects:

18.Courage Portrait

Purpose of Project:

Each of us has courage in us. Each of us knows what moments we must draw on this resource, whether others can see it or not. This is the opportunity to be aware of our own courage and document it, claim it and support our ability to be courageous. **Courage doesn't mean that we aren't afraid**. It actually means that we are afraid and we become big enough to be able to be afraid and still do what we need to do or be who we need to be. **We become bigger than the fear**. It becomes something that can pass through us instead of stopping us. Then we continue with our lives. Speak about this to the students.

Process:

GUIDE ARTISTS IN THE FOLLOWING STEPS:

1. Using the oil pastels use either your favorite color or a color that represents **COURAGE** for you and draw a pattern around all of you. It could be as simple as a thick line, or it could as complicated as a boundary of thorns or ocean waves or even a line of barking dogs or vibrating lines out in a rainbow! Take your time. Think about how courageous you are as you do this. Remember all the times you were courageous. Afraid, but still doing what you needed to do or being who you needed to be. *(Fig. 2)*

2. Using the pencil, draw the fear. It could be something like a monster or even something real that you are afraid of. Or it could just be a dot or a scribble. Place it anywhere in the art that you think best. Over your chest? In your head? Outside of you entirely? *(Fig. 3)*

3. Feel the courage that is yours and sign.

PREP

- Photograph students (see *Working with Photographs* in *Chapter 7*, pages 96-97).
- Print/copy one "regular" photo per student on heavy cardstock. *(Fig. 1)*

MATERIALS

- "Regular" photo of each student printed on cardstock
- Oil pastels
- Pencil

BOOKS

Prietita and the Ghost Woman
by Gloria Anzuldua
In this story Prietita ventures out into dangerous and forbidden territory in search of a much needed healing herb. She keeps herself strong and moving forward, even when she's afraid.

I Frame Myself Step-by-Step

Fig. 1⌐   Fig. 2⌐

Fig. 3⌐

Fig. 4⌐

Fig. 5⌐

Classroom Notes:

What I learned from doing the project myself:

What did or didn't work in the classroom:

How I would change or modify the project:

Inspirations, new ideas & directions, other projects:

19. I Frame Myself
Word Window

Purpose of Project:

All of the **CLAIMING FACE** projects are geared toward simple opportunities to know ourselves and **claim our experience**. This project allows us to clearly state things for ourselves that we feel and things that we like.

Process:

GUIDE ARTISTS IN THE FOLLOWING STEPS:

1. Make sure the piece of color construction paper is at least 4 inches wider on all sides than the center image.

2. Depending on the age of the students:

- Fold color paper in half long ways and line up half of photo in center and trace. Then cut out a window ½ inch smaller than the outline of the photo to create your window, place photo in frame and glue or tape into place.

- OR glue photo down in center of color paper.

3. Write or draw what you like, what you love, how you feel, what's important to you, etc…around the frame.

4. Write the title of the project "I Frame Myself" across top or bottom of your piece.

5. Decorate photo with color, glitter glue or other fanciful additions.

6. Sign your work.

PREP

- Collect photos from students or Photograph students (see *Working with Photographs* in *Chapter 7*, pages 96-97).

  Maya Tip: *I suggest using their school photo for this one. These are often very posed and formal and this would give the opportunity to add more dimension to it.*

- Print/copy one photo per student on heavy cardstock.

MATERIALS

- Any photo of each student
- Large color construction paper
- Scissors
- Markers of any kind
- Glue Stick

Optional:
- Glitter Glue and other objects

BOOKS

Just Like Me: Stories and Self-portraits by Fourteen Artists specifically my portrait framed by words.

Touch Your Face Step-by-Step

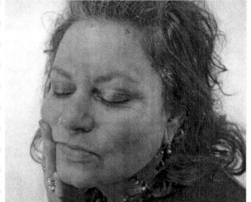

Fig. 1

Fig. 2

Fig. 3

Classroom Notes:

What I learned from doing the project myself:

What did or didn't work in the classroom:

How I would change or modify the project:

Inspirations, new ideas & directions, other projects:

20. Touch Your Face
Portrait

Purpose of Project:

This project **expands our ways of knowing**. Often our drawing becomes prescribed, especially with faces! Two eyes, nose, mouth, head, etc… We do not search for our face, we draw the nose we know how to draw. It may be our nose or it may simply be how we were taught to draw a nose at some point. Through the process of this project, we experience ourselves in a more authentic way through touch and exploration like in the *Imagine* exercise in *Chapter 1, pg. 20.*

Process:

1. Specifically instruct everyone to **FORGET THEY KNOW WHAT THEY LOOK LIKE!**

2. Have artists close their eyes and touch their face. Touch every part, even nostrils! Pretend they've never seen themselves and they want to know the shapes of their face. *(Fig. 1 & 2)*

3. Ask questions: *Are your lips wide or thin? Is your forehead tall or short? Can you feel the corners of your eyes? Do they tip up or down or are they straight? What about your cheeks? Can you feel the cheek bone or are they full like apples?*

GUIDE ARTISTS IN THE FOLLOWING STEPS:

4. Begin by just scribbling how your face feels. Let's say you have big apple cheeks. Begin by scribbling round circles like apples where your cheeks are. Imagine using your pencil to sculpt your face. No perfect straight lines. Try not to lift your pencil off the paper and keep feeling your face and trying to scribble the shapes you feel. *(Fig. 3)*

5. Draw your whole head.

6. Sign your work.

MATERIALS

- Pencil
- One blank sheet of paper per artwork

BOOKS

Please don't reference a book for this project
In this project the student and their experience is the only reference.

Space or Place Step-by-Step

Fig. 1

Fig. 2

Fig. 3

Fig. 4

Classroom Notes:

What I learned from doing the project myself:

What did or didn't work in the classroom:

How I would change or modify the project:

Inspirations, new ideas & directions, other projects:

21. Self-Portrait
as Space or Place

EXPLORE

Purpose of Project:

In *My Colors, My World* the little girl finds herself in her world as the Hot Pink of the sunset. In *My Very Own Room* the little girl creates her own room so she can expand and be more herself. This projects opens up the possibilities of where we may find the reflection of our self, and how we create our world as a reflection of our self.

Process:

MATERIALS

1. Choose the materials for this project as a class. Provide 3 or more options, for example Crayons, Oil Pastels or Cut Paper and take a vote.

GUIDE ARTISTS IN THE FOLLOWING STEPS:

2. Draw yourself as something you relate to in nature, You could draw yourself strong like a tree, or wild or even calm like a river. *(Fig. 2)*

> *Maya Tip: for example, in My Colors, My World I am the sunset because of the gorgeous colors as big as the sky.*

3. Or draw yourself as a bedroom, a home, a school, an art studio. Include colors, furniture, books, art supplies, clothes? *(Fig. 3)*

4. Sign your work.

• Choose materials as a class. Voting on materials provides the students the chance to know what they like, but be flexible in adapting to whatever material is voted for by the class.

> *Maya Tip: I've done this project with a big piece of paper and crayons. But at one school some of the students used it to create dioramas of their own space.*

BOOKS

My Very Own Room
          by Amada Irma Perez

My Colors, My World
          by Maya Gonzalez

No One Can See Step-by-Step

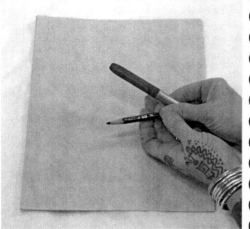

Fig. 1

Fig. 2

Fig. 3

Classroom Notes:

What I learned from doing the project myself:

What did or didn't work in the classroom:

How I would change or modify the project:

Inspirations, new ideas & directions, other projects:

22. What No One Can See Portrait

FUNDAMENTALS #8 EXPAND

Purpose of Project:

What can you tell by looking at me? Can you tell who I love? Can you tell what frightens me? What about where I was born? Or what I do in my spare time? Who we are is layered. Through this project we can bring parts of our self that we may hide or don't publicly acknowledge together with the parts we love to share with folks. This creates room for us to be more present. Often we are not aware of what we don't show because we are too busy paying attention to what we do show. It's not as important to include in your picture something that you don't show, it could be that part still doesn't want to show. What's important is the experience of knowing that you can make art that shows something that's usually invisible. It **supports the relationship between the artist and the creative process**. Art is someplace you can go and completely be yourself. You can even have art, and kids often do, that no one else can see or only certain folks can see. It's yours. Completely. This project also allows a more multi-dimensional perception of others. What can't we see when we look at someone else?

Process:

1. Explore what we can and can't see by looking at each other.

GUIDE ARTISTS IN THE FOLLOWING STEPS:

2. With one medium, like the pencil, draw a picture of yourself. *(Fig. 2)*

3. With another medium, like watercolors or watercolor pencils, draw onto your picture something about you that someone can't see by looking at you. *(Fig. 3)*

4. Sign your work.

MATERIALS

• Two mediums: Pencils and pastels. Watercolors and crayons. Or.. *(Fig. 1)*

• One blank sheet of paper per artwork

BOOKS

Just Like Me: Stories and Self-Portraits by Fourteen Artists
In my portrait in this book I paint an unusual experience I had as a child that no one can see.

Tell a Tale Step-by-Step

Fig. 1

Fig. 2

Fig. 3

Classroom Notes:

What I learned from doing the project myself:

What did or didn't work in the classroom:

How I would change or modify the project:

Inspirations, new ideas & directions, other projects:

23. Tell a Tale
Without Words

EXPRESS

Purpose of Project:

Open a book. Through looking at the pictures alone, see how much of the story you can gather without reading the words. **Sometimes we don't have words** for what we're experiencing. Either because we can't yet understand or speak about something that is going on, or because there literally aren't words to convey what we're experiencing. Creativity is a great tool to process, synthesize and express multiple layers of experience. We use a different part of our brain when we are creative. This increases our internal resources and our ability to develop more advanced thought processes.

Process:

GUIDE ARTISTS IN THE FOLLOWING STEPS:

1. If you needed to tell a story about yourself or something that happened to you, but you could only use art, what would you create? What story would you tell? What images would you use to tell it? Tell a story with pictures.

2. Cut out images from the magazines to help you tell your story. *(Fig. 1)*

Maya Tip: Look at how I used keys, Milagros and the shawl in Nana's Big Surprise to tell part of the story.

3. Draw parts of your story adding images to convey different parts of the tale. *(Fig. 2)*

4. When ready, glue your images down. *(Fig. 3)*

5. Sign your work.

PREP

• Collect various magazines

MATERIALS

• Magazines - always as many different kinds as possible
• Scissors
• Glue Stick
• Drawing material: Pencils, Markers, Oil Pastels, etc.
• One blank sheet of paper per artwork

BOOKS

Nana's Big Surprise
        by Amada Irma Perez
How much of the story can you tell just by looking at a book? If you follow the images of keys, Nana's heart, and her shawl what are they telling you about the story?

River Loves Me Step-by-Step

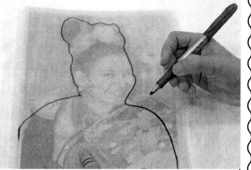

Fig. 1

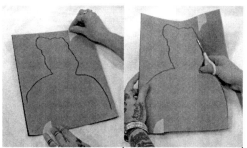

Fig. 2   Fig. 3

Fig. 4   Fig. 5

Fig. 6

Classroom Notes:

What I learned from doing the project myself:

What did or didn't work in the classroom:

How I would change or modify the project:

Inspirations, new ideas & directions, other projects:

24. I Know the River Loves Me

EXPAND

Purpose of Project:

In *I Know the River Loves Me*, I share that not only can we find ourselves in nature like in *My Colors, My World*, but that we can have a relationship with her. I believe this is important because there are times when we will not easily fit into a new culture or the power dynamics that affect our lives, but through our awareness of and relationship with nature, we can know that we belong where we are and we are loved at all times. Nature travels with us. It is the greater reality of the world and is without language, a neutral place where we all live, beyond stress and beyond the dynamics of culture, community or family. Even in urban settings nature is all around us. For example, the sky is always above us and flowers grow small and weedy no matter where we are. When we see ourselves in nature, love her and notice the ways that she loves us back, it gives us a way to engage with the world around us.

PREP

- Photograph students (see *Working with Photographs* in *Chapter 7*, pages 96-97).
- Print/copy one "regular" image per student on heavy cardstock paper. *(Fig. 1)*
- This project offers **opportunity for greater study**. Connect this to studying nature, like rivers and oceans or fish and animals.

Process: GUIDE ARTISTS IN THE FOLLOWING STEPS:

1. Tape tracing paper over photo of self and trace around outer edge of head and shoulders. *(Fig. 1)*

2. Remove tracing paper from photo, tape tracing paper onto black paper and cut around the outline. *(Fig. 2 & 3)* This leaves you with a black cut out of your silhouette.

3. Glue your black silhouette onto a piece of colored paper. *(Fig. 4)*

4. Think about a good friend in nature and draw this onto your silhouette. For example, waves from a river or branches and leaves from a tree. Then draw the surrounding environment around your silhouette. For example the grass at the river's edge or the birds flying around the tree. *(Fig. 5)*

5. Cut your face out of your photo and glue onto your silhouette where your face would go. *(Fig. 6)*

6. Decorate your face to match the rest of your art.

7. Sign your work.

MATERIALS

- "Regular" photo of each student
- Oil Pastels and Markers
- One black and one colored sheet of construction paper per artwork
- Scissors
- Tracing Paper
- Glue Stick

BOOKS

Animal Poems of the Iguazu
    by Francisco Alarcon

I Know the River Loves Me
    by Maya Gonzalez

Seeing Through Step-by-Step

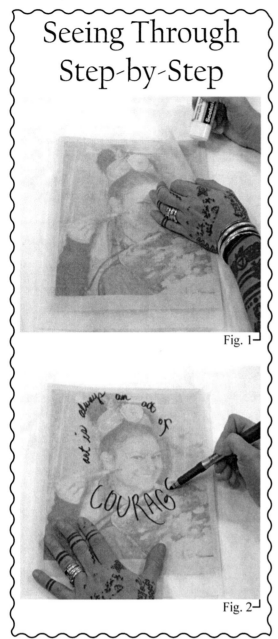

Fig. 1

Fig. 2

Classroom Notes:

What I learned from doing the project myself:

What did or didn't work in the classroom:

How I would change or modify the project:

Inspirations, new ideas & directions, other projects:

25. Seeing Through Words

EXPAND

<table>
</table>

Purpose of Project:

The purpose of this project is to continue to play with who we are. While it is good to know what we love, the world around us, our feelings, we are much more than all of that. We are something deep and simple. We are our self. We are not what we believe or what others believe about us. We are not what happens to us. This project allows us to toy with separating what we believe from who we are. We can choose the words and the ideas we want to believe in, but they are not who we are. In this project the students are literally making a work of art of themselves looking through their own thoughts.

Process:

1. Don't explain this project too much. Just encourage artists to find words that they would like to see in front of their eyes.

GUIDE ARTISTS IN THE FOLLOWING STEPS:

2. Tape, glue or staple the tracing paper to the top of your portrait. *(Fig. 1)*

3. Write single words or a quote or a list of heroes or a poem or whatever you need on the tracing paper over your face. The words could completely cover your face underneath the tracing paper, or just your eyes or your mouth or could be kept along the edges, off the face area. *(Fig. 2)*

4. Sign your work.

PREP

- Photograph students (see *Working with Photographs* in *Chapter 7*, pages 96-97).
- Print/copy one "regular" photo per student on heavy cardstock.

MATERIALS

- "Regular" photo of each student printed on cardstock
- Tracing Paper
- Pen or Marker
- Tape, Glue Stick, or Stapler

BOOKS

No Book

All of Me
Step-by-Step

Fig. 1

Fig. 2

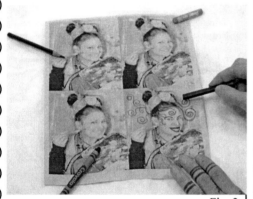

Fig. 3

Classroom Notes:

What I learned from doing the project myself:

What did or didn't work in the classroom:

How I would change or modify the project:

Inspirations, new ideas & directions, other projects:

26. All of Me
Portrait/Portrait/Portrait/Portrait

EXPRESS

Purpose of Project:

As we have explored, there are many aspects to ourselves and there are many ways to create. Look at the art in *Just Like Me*. What is George Littlechild showing us through presenting himself 4 times. They're all photographs of George, but each is different. He says, *"My looks change according to my mood. That's why I made these four different portraits. It took me many years to accept my features. Then one day I had to love myself just the way I am."* And what about Daryl Wells? She is exploring and expanding how skin color is represented. Does her image feel different in different mediums? She says, *"When I was growing up I didn't understand why the crayon labeled 'flesh' in my crayon box wasn't the color my skin...everybody's skin has many colors in it and the way people look has a lot to do with how they're feeling at the time."*

 **PREP**

- Photograph students (see *Working with Photographs* in *Chapter 7*, pages 96-97).
- Print/copy 4 of the same photo per student on heavy cardstock according to options: *(Fig. 1)*

    Option 1: Print the 4 photos each at 8½ x 11, if desks are large enough and have space to display.

    Option 2: Print all 4 photos onto an 8½ x 11 page.

Process:

GUIDE ARTISTS IN THE FOLLOWING STEPS:

1. Show four different aspects of yourself that are all here at once.

2. *If Option 2:* fold paper with 4 photos on it in half one way then in half the other way to divide the 4 images. Unfold and lay flat.

3. For each photo, in each square or on each page, use a different art material, for example colored pencils on one photo, pastels on another, charcoal on another and crayons on the last one.

4. Sign your work.

 **MATERIALS**

- Photo of each student (per Option 1 or 2 under Prep)
- 4 different mediums: for example, crayons, oil pastels, watercolor pencil, chalk pastel

 **BOOKS**

Just Like Me: Stories and Self-Portraits by Fourteen Artists specifically George Littlechild and Daryl Wells

KEYS TO REMEMBER FROM CHAPTER 9:

• Use *Chapter 7, Materials, Display & Storage* and *Chapter 8, Books: Behind the Story* as references when completing the projects to add depth and encourage multiple ways of knowing.

• When speaking about the art your students create, refer to *Chapter 4*, specifically the section, *Presence in the Classroom*.

• Remember the 6 project categories: **Reflection, Express, Explore, Empower, Expand** and **Freedom** and how they relate to **THE 3 RULES**. (*pg. 125*)

• The curriculum is designed to build on the experience of previous projects so if possible, do the Full Schedule.

• Choose a project schedule, Fundamentals or Claiming Face Full schedule, or choose individual projects according to what you feel your class needs. Use the planning tools to help you. (*pgs. 125-127*)

• Projects take about 40 mins to an hour but can be expanded or broken up if desired.

• Familiarize yourself with the symbols to make implementing the projects easier.

• Print enough copies of photos and handouts for the school year according to your desired project schedule. Here is a quick list of photos/handouts needed based on class size of 30 students:

Fundamentals Schedule:
  15 - Making Face handout #1 on cardstock
  15 - Making Face handout #2 on cardstock
  30 - Rule #1 handout on cardstock
  30 - Frida handout on cardstock
  30 - Rule #2 handout on cardstock
  30 - Rule #3 handout on cardstock
  "Regular" photo (1 of each student) = 30 student photos on cardstock
  "Wild" photo (1 of each student) = 30 student photos on cardstock

CLAIMING FACE **Full Schedule:**
  September - January (First photo shoot of students)
    15 - Making Face handout #1 on cardstock
    15 - Making Face handout #2 on cardstock
    30 - Frida handout on cardstock
    "Regular" photo (1 of each student) = 30 student photos on cardstock
    "Wild" photo (1 of each student) = 30 student photos on cardstock
    30 - Rule #1 handout on cardstock
    30 - Rule #2 handout on cardstock
  January - June (Second photo shoot of students)
    30 - Rule #3 handout on cardstock
    "Regular" photo (4 of each student) = 120 student photos on cardstock
    All of Me Option 1: 4 "Regular" photo on 1 page of cardstock for each student = 30
    All of Me Option 2: "Regular" photo (4 of each student) = 120 on cardstock

***Note that this is just the minimum, you may want extra copies on hand

Imagine

Expansion

In Closing......

Breathe in deeply. Feel your weight upon your chair. Sense your body supported by the chair, the chair supported by the floor, the floor supported by the structure of the building, the building supported by the earth. Visualize how much support is involved in you sitting here now. Wood, metal, earth. You are supported completely.

As you sit here solid and strong, you sense a warm wind. At first it is like a soft caress across your skin. It warms you and you relax into all your support. The wind grows stronger and lifts your hair and the edges of your clothes. Breathe in this warm wind and feel your insides warm. The wind grows stronger and you imagine leaves blowing, branches bending. You remain fully supported and solid, but you bend some in the wind. Because you are so strong and supported, you can bend with the warm wind, move gently like the branches of a tree.

The wind continues to grow in strength. The stronger it gets, it seems the more solid and stable you become. It is as if a part of you is reaching down through the chair, the floor and the foundation of the building deep into the earth like a root. Once you reach the earth, this part of you spreads out like a root. You sense the deep comfort of the dark earth and burrow deeply and finger out. Connected deeply to the earth you feel even more stable in yourself. You sense your trunk thick and solid. Your branches reach out wide, but bend in the strong wind that blows warmly all around you. It is as if the warm wind is embracing you even as it moves you. You realize that you have leaves and you can feel their tips shiver and shake with the wind. As a tree you and the wind are dancing. One wind, one tree in perfect motion. This way, then that way.

As you become more aware of your dance as a tree with the wind, you see that everything in the environment around you is lifting up and flying about. Things you thought were immovable are up in the air, turning, reorienting. Things that you thought were light and flighty are doing their own beautiful dance high above the tips of your branches, up, up in the air. Just as it seems that everything has been rearranged, reorganized by this great warm wind, it begins to blow slightly less and less. All that was in the air begins to come down, slowly, until this and that begins to settle softly onto the ground again. Everything that should be on the earth is back down again, but now in slightly different ways and places.

The wind fades out completely. All that is left is a warm feeling. You look around and see that everything in your environment has somehow been naturally rearranged in a more perfect manner. As if it was a highly intelligent wind that came through and gently reorganized everything to better suit you, your work, your life, your relationships, your place in the world. You cannot understand how this has happened, but it feels so right and you feel so solid and stable, you simply relax.

When you are ready, pick up your pencil or pen and draw your roots, your trunk your branches and leaves.

Use the following page to draw........

1 Do you have a favorite tree? Where does it live? Do you ever watch it move in the wind?

Reflect

2 If a highly intelligent wind blew through your life, what would it naturally reorganize? How would you and your life feel if this area of your life was reorganized?

3 Can you imagine continuing to use creativity as a tool to know yourself? Can you imagine continuing to use creativity as a tool to empower your students?

4 What do you imagine would be the effects of engaging with the CLAIMING FACE curriculum for a whole year for you? For your students?

5 What do you imagine would be the effects of engaging with the CLAIMING FACE curriculum for two years? Three years? A lifetime?

6 What might be the long term effects of knowing yourself deeply? What might be the long term effects of feeling that you are an empowered creative person who can trust your own knowing? What would this world look like if this were the norm?

Draw it! Claim it! Draw it! Claim it!

Draw it! Claim it! Draw it! Claim it!

Draw it! Claim it!

"Making oneself visible changes the world as we know it."

Afterword

Living the Curriculum

As I said at the opening of *Chapter 1*, I can consciously trace the origin of the CLAIMING FACE curriculum back to my childhood. At age 4, I created much needed reflection by drawing my face into the backs of books. In **On My Block** I tell a story about how at age 7, I felt truly seen for myself when I received my first real art materials. When I moved to Oregon at 13, I created an extensive cartoon series with characters based on me, and my father as a child. Ironically they had facial features, but no outline of the head to contain them. In my early 20's I began in earnest creating art as a tool to affirm and claim myself, my face.

As I've gotten older I've learned that there is always something to learn in this world in relation to claiming face. And thankfully the inner teacher, Creativity always has something to teach. What I began at 4 seems more relevant than ever now. My lesson, my experience, my knowing, my self has deepened by engaging with creativity and claiming. I look back at images of me as a child and I can see the wisdom I had then. I am still that same person, only more so.

I have learned that while this is my lesson and journey, it is not mine alone. It is a planetary journey. It is your journey and it is a child's journey. As much as I love to study quantum physics, ancient history, somatic psychology and even fashion, art is my path. I see now that it is only through the deep study and teaching of the freedom and authenticity of creativity that I can reach out and access what is at the heart of each of us. I am coming to accept that teaching is important to me because I have a deep commitment to supporting others like me to be our most true and creatively empowered selves. Claiming ourselves through the power of creativity holds a gentle, simple trend toward change for our world. In my imagination I see what a world looks like where each of us knows ourselves from the inside out and celebrates who we truly are. It is a valuable and worthy vision to work toward. It begins with the self. When we change ourselves, we change everything.

So this is my life. What does it mean to live this curriculum, to live as an artist? It's difficult for me to say in some ways. I have to be honest, it has been fabulously, excruciatingly challenging for me to articulate my thoughts and share what I live in this book. I am an artist. I can talk up a storm, but I have a very idiosyncratic way of speaking that I've tried to "translate" to be more easily understood. And besides that, I truly love to spend a lot of time alone plumbing my private thoughts while drawing or painting. I imagine I would be living a different life if I had never gone into the schools as a children's book illustrator. If I had never met all of the many amazing children

"my self has deepened by engaging with creativity…"

there and started sharing with them what I learned as a child using art as a tool to claim my face. But this led me to see first hand how CLAIMING FACE can affect and serve our children. I can't ignore that.

So I come forward with not only my curriculum, but also with myself. My work started with myself and I believe because of that I have a greater depth with the curriculum and can share with deep insight and empathy. When I go into the schools or even speak at conferences I hold a strong focus on children and what is most relevant in relation to them. But here I want to share some of how living the curriculum has served me as an adult. I am teaching you now and I teach what I've learned.

Through art I celebrate and I struggle. Art has helped me to claim myself through numerous experiences. Through my 20's and 30's art helped me negotiate the effects of childhood incest, being disowned by my family for being queer and living through and eventually leaving an abusive 15 year relationship. In my 40's I used art to endure and overcome a long term serious illness as my large 5'x6' paintings shrank to 3"x3" pencil drawings. I use art to understand and express my current experiences through a complicated co-parenting situation and come into more of my power as a mature woman. Art is always with me. It helps me to know myself through challenging lessons. It is also there to help me express my unspeakable joy of being alive, my great love of nature, the profound ecstasy of spirit, the deep joy of parenting and finally the amazing feeling of finally being loved well and being able to love back wholly.

It is tricky business in this world to know yourself fully and be who you really are from the inside out, but art is a great container. For me it's the only way I can mediate between my inside and outside experience. It's a life of meditation in a way. I used to say that I was an art nun. Creativity keeps me focused and devoted and in constant lesson around letting go, trust and courage, but also curiosity, freedom and expansion. I can say with all the power of my being now that I love my life. And I am wildly devoted to my teacher, Creativity. It's clear that creativity and art mean a great deal to me and I immensely appreciate the time you've taken with me.

ENGAGING MY BIGGER, SMARTER CREATIVE BRAIN

I create a great deal of everything, including art. I have short intense seasons on occasion when I produce art for a children's book, but the vast majority of art that I create is solely for me. As an adult, I have focused a great deal on art, but between the ages of 13 and 23 I wanted nothing more than to be a writer. I went to college for creative writing, but through that

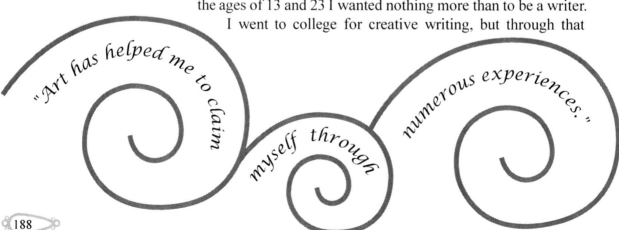

"Art has helped me to claim myself through numerous experiences."

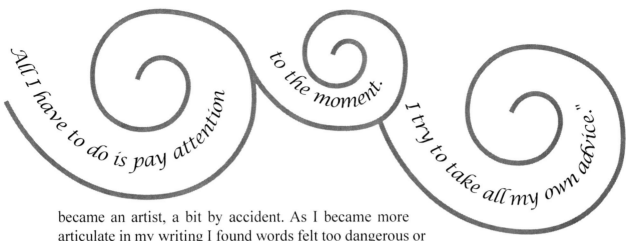

All I have to do is pay attention to the moment. I try to take all my own advice."

became an artist, a bit by accident. As I became more articulate in my writing I found words felt too dangerous or explicit. Still filled with the need to express and integrate I turned again toward creating art. This shift showed me that the creative form can be anything. Sometimes its writing, but it can be painting. It can also be sewing or crocheting or cooking or parenting, even driving. If I pay attention I notice everything is creative.

When I frame all of my activities as creative, the tiniest to the biggest decisions and actions show me myself. What is important to me? What is my overall style toward life, energy, activity? This frame supports me to stay fluid, open, trusting like I do when I'm making art. It holds true that if I pay attention to the moment and let go, I will find my way to do absolutely anything I need to do.

At times I am my most uncomfortable when something new or different is trying to come through creatively. It can feel akin to irritation, like things aren't quite right; drawing or however I'm making art is just too hard. Everything feels too big or too much and I'm plagued with the question, why do I do this? I challenge myself to just notice the discomfort and the irritation and trytrytry to relax into it. I don't think something great is going to come through. I hear myself thinking that engaging with creativity kinda sucks. I keep letting go and trusting even though I'm having these thoughts. I remind myself that I don't have to do anything. All I have to do is pay attention to the moment. I try to take all my own advice. Remember what I've learned. Sometimes I can only do that by remembering what I teach.

There are times when all I can do to engage the creative energy is organize my pens in color sequences or sort my art paper. I engage with the peripherals of creating. Then at some point, I have this funny feeling like I really want to draw. It might not work right off the bat, I just keep playing. It's usually important to not have a plan. Just have the feeling that I want to draw. Then, slowly, connections start coming through that I had never thought of before. If I surrender to the moment I often end up drawing things I never would have thought of with my tiny, regular, day brain. It's like my bigger, smarter, creative brain has kicked in. Sometimes it feels like I'm watching my hands make drawings that tell me stories, stories about crazy deep parts of myself that have no words. I feel like I can't create fast enough. Three drawings will all pop out in a few days and I can barely keep up with them. I HAVE to draw every spare moment I have. I make more time if I have to by staying up late into the night drawing.

When I'm done it can be years before I fully understand the depth and breadth of what I'm telling myself about my own self. This is why I create. Many things in life are uncomfortable. It is almost always a challenge to engage with the unknown, especially within ourselves. But through this process, I have come to know and integrate things I never dreamed I could deal with. Haunts and ghosts, insecurities and fears, angers and hurts, but also deep spiritual truths and immense joy. All this has found face in my work. In creating and reflecting upon them I have grown stronger, more resilient, more compassionate, wiser, and trusting of process, of living, of being. I have learned to listen to myself, especially parts of myself that seem only to come out when I make art. I feel that my art knows me better than I do. That's why I have learned to pay close attention to it. It's also part of why I want to share it with children and with you.

I love fine art. I use it to add dimension and support integration of my experiences, emotions and thoughts. I generally draw either myself, an aspect of myself or a representation of something I'm learning. This is true even when I'm working on a children's book that I did not write. I work with authors whose stories are resonant with my own. This way I can stay true to how art works best for me. I can explore, discover and express myself through another's story or poem.

When I'm doing art for a new children's book I like to court courage. I use it as an excuse to try something unknown to me, something I don't technically know how to do. I have an idea, but not too much. I do this in part because I think it's an amazing feeling to have an idea and make it happen when there's a lot of unknown to it. I appreciate that's how children feel all the time. Of course, once I start working on the book I inevitably hit walls. I don't know what I'm doing and that can feel hard and confusing. It's not the same as doing something I have already mastered and feel confident about. So I love it, but it gives me the opportunity to remind myself A LOT about the *3RD RULE*. This keeps me honest and in touch with what I know to be true about art. It reminds me to be present and curious. I explore and wonder and realize how much I don't know, and how much I could learn!

I've found that being open and sitting in the unknown is a bit like life. Art-Life-Art-Life. It's all the same to me. **We are all artists, all the time. How beautiful is that?**

"I have learned to listen to myself, especially parts of myself that seem only to come out when I make art."

Love,
maya

RESOURCES

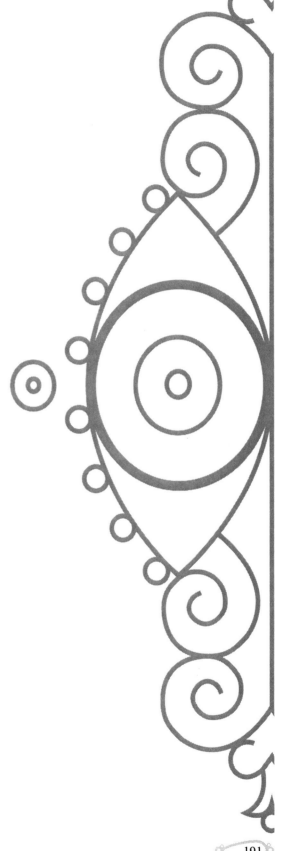

The CLAIMING FACE Please! Cheat ^ Sheet

KEYS TO REMEMBER FROM CHAPTER 1:

- Our face communicates something about us that as children we may not understand.
- We sense that we belong and are valued in our culture when we see ourselves in the media in our world.
- Graffiti that impacted me: "a people should not long for their own image."
- I realized that if we don't want to long for our own image, we are going to have to create it for ourselves.
- CLAIMING FACE means to value ourselves for who we really are.
- The Educator's Guide is divided into three parts: *Inside*-development and philosophies, *Outside*-setting up the physical environment and *Process*-26 projects based on self-portraiture.
- The curriculum is for:
    - Anyone who is curious (you DO NOT have to consider yourself an artist or feel creative in any way).
    - Educators wishing to increase the cultural capacity of their class.
    - Educators wishing to empower their selves.
    - Educators wishing to empower their students.
    - Educators working with ESL students.
- You can choose how much time you want to work with the Guide from deep study to immediate support.
- The Guide is designed to be easy to use.
- Familiarize yourself with the different symbols to provide an at-a-glance reference to different parts of the curriculum (see Symbols Legend on page 17).
- The curriculum is not tied to teaching art skills, meeting standards or other academic subjects so that it can be personally claimed by each student.
- The CLAIMING FACE curriculum can be blended with academic subjects if so desired.
- Whether it is tied to other subjects or not, it will support students personally and academically.

KEYS TO REMEMBER FROM CHAPTER 2:

- The real power of creativity is being able to use it to empower our self, for example through creating our own reflection.
- When we are reflected in our world, we sense that we belong.
- Creating reflections of ourselves allows us to reflect upon and better know ourselves.

- It's valuable to understand the underlying effects of invisibility and institutionalized racism.
- Witnessing is the dynamic process that occurs when we are seen by another or by our self.
- We change things by observing them.
- *Universal Reflection*: reflection becomes universal when it is not dependent on image but on action between two or more people.
- Creating reflection through action equalizes student and educator and helps to dismantle and balance power structures that exist in our current culture.
- When you engage with the curriculum for yourself:
  - You create your own reflection
  - You come to know yourself more deeply
  - You provide *Universal Reflection* for your students
  - You demonstrate the equality between you and your students
  - You serve as a model to witness and emulate
  - You learn, you grow, bigger, stronger, you become even more fabulous!

Keys to Remember from Chapter 3:

- The curriculum is designed to support freedom coming up slowly over time so that energy and our ability to hold it can build steadily.
- Being "in on something" with the children, like a joke, for example the "Bob" Trick, or taking a "risk" together, for example drawing something you're "not supposed to," is a way to show that you as the educator are on their side.
- Presence is fundamental to the CLAIMING FACE curriculum and is a primary tool for dealing with energy of all kinds.
- Don't push energy down. We want it to flow.
- Energy, whether creative, emotional, physical, or other, naturally rises and naturally falls.
- I use water as a metaphor to understand the nature of energy and how it moves.
- The purpose of some of the projects is to make judgment visible and help remove external influences in order to come to our own conclusions and understandings about our self.
- The most powerful thing you can do as an educator is be yourself.
- When we change, we change everything.

Keys to Remember from Chapter 4:

What does being *Present* mean

- Being *Present* means that we are aware of ourself as much as possible especially our body.
- Body feelings are often attached to emotional feelings.

What does being *Present* do

- Supports energy flow.
- Changes what you observe.
- Allows you to know yourself more.

Being *Present* with Self

- Make internal space with your imagination.
- Remove judgement.
- Pay attention to your body feelings.
- Refer to the exercise on page 50 to practice presence with yourself. Experiment anytime during the day. There is no set duration.
- Beginning with yourself creates an internal pattern that is easier for your students to emulate.

Being *Present* with Students/Hard Feelings

- Stop fully with each student.
- Pay attention to the students facial expressions and how they hold their body.
- Remind your student of the *3RD RULE, "ART IS ALWAYS AND ACT OF COURAGE."*

Being *Present* in the Classroom and with Art

- Students never have to speak about their art, they can always pass.
- Focus on physical descriptions of art.
- Speak respectfully about self, art, students, and facing the unknown.
- Allow everyone to speak about their own art.
- *EVERYONE IS AN ARTIST.* Don't single anyone out as "The Artist" in the class.
- Create a specific setting to share art.
- Projects are never graded.

Being *Present* with *The 3 Rules*

- Post the *RULES* in the classroom.
- Refer to the *RULES* frequently.
- Engage the students in determining how to follow the *RULES* as a class.

KEYS TO REMEMBER FROM CHAPTER 5:

- Many outside influences affect our creative expression: family, school, religion, ethnic and social ties, gender, the era we live in.
- Be curious to see what could be affecting expression.
- Girls are expected to express "pretty" and "nice" things. Boys are expected to take up more space and express more, as long as it is not too nice or pretty.
- Pay attention to princesses and trucks as much as more individual and articulate imagery.
- Stressed out children demonstrate the power of the curriculum first.

- Ways to let go and express emotion in art:
  - use your body to hold the emotion.
  - use a symbol to represent experience or emotion.
- Support all children for their **human potential** first and foremost.
- Life skills supersede art skills.
- Art skills are more likely to develop but are not a focus with this curriculum.
- Resources for students who want to pursue fine art:
  - go to the library to research art, artists and role models.
  - go to public art programs in libraries, museums and recreation centers.
  - make an artist's notebook.

KEYS TO REMEMBER FROM CHAPTER 6:

- *RULE #1: EVERYONE IS AN ARTIST:*
  - Reflection: self as creative.
  - Express: expanded reflection gives new purpose as artist to express.
- Polka Dot Theory: even a polka dot shows something about ourselves.
- *RULE #2: THERE IS NEVER A RIGHT OR WRONG WAY TO MAKE ART:*
  - Explore: we are free to explore without the pressure of judgement.
  - Empower: we become our own authority.
- Boss of Me: only we can know, be, and express ourselves.
- *RULE #3: ART IS ALWAYS AN ACT OF COURAGE.*
  - Freedom: free to have all feelings.
  - Expand: more space for our feelings to move and expand.
- Mistakes and courage are a part of art: not framing things as mistakes but as moments of courage supports students to be curious and open to what could happen next.

KEYS TO REMEMBER FROM CHAPTER 7:

Using the Materials

- If you're getting dirty, you know you're making art.
- Using materials like Charcoal and Oil Pastels make a big difference in instilling confidence in children that they are artists.
- Familiarize yourself with the materials for more freedom and confidence to explore.
- Much of the art in the projects is linked to art in a related book, combining literacy with art.

Working with Photographs

- Choose the photo style most convenient to you.
- Photos don't have to be perfect, just need a good likeness of each student.
- Use a flash and shoot only head and shoulders against a plain background.

- Two shots per student, one regular and one wild.
- Take photos twice a year if possible, once in October and again in January/February.
- Copy and store as many photos as you need for the school year or semester to make project preparation simpler.
- Always print on a heavy paper like cardstock.

Classroom Set Up

- Support flow through simple and predictable set up and clean up practices.
- Involve students in every aspect of making art, set up, clean up, display and storage.
- Have accessible art materials to use during students' free time.
- Store art materials in reach of students in clearly marked boxes.
- Keep clean up easy by covering the desks or have an art board for each student.

Display

- Gallery: have a specially designated area to serve as the self-portrait gallery.
- Curator: taking down and putting up new work is a special job.
- Art openings: share work in larger and larger communities.
- Treat work respectfully.

Storage

- Have safe places for things to dry if wet.
- Cover art made with pastels or charcoal with an extra sheet of paper or plastic before storing.
- Have a place to store completed work.
- Create a portfolio.

KEYS TO REMEMBER FROM CHAPTER 8:

- *Just Like Me:* An unexplainable experience about light and the heart.
- *On My Block:* Recovery from a serious accident and the love of art that came with that experience.
- *My Colors, My World:* Finding color in the world after an experience has turned the world colorless. Turn the book upside down to see the blind faces on the wind swirls.
- *I Know the River Loves Me:* The river told me the story.
- *Laughing Tomatoes and Other Spring Poems:* There's a secret hidden in the art on the Laughing Tomato poem.
- *Angels Ride Bikes and Other Fall Poems:* Look for the lines in the art where I glued down the photos. Can you cheat in art?
- *Animal Poems of the Iguazu:* The animals were painted as a sign of respect. The rest of the book is made of cut paper to make the environments for the animals.
- *My Very Own Room:* See how to use oil pastels by looking at the art.
- *Nana's Big Surprise:* Look for the keys and how the heart moves and the shawl transforms throughout the art of the book.

Cheat Sheet

Keys to Remember from Chapter 9:

- Use *Chapter 7, Materials, Display & Storage* and *Chapter 8, Books: Behind the Story* as references when completing the projects to add depth and encourage multiple ways of knowing.

- When speaking about the art your students create, refer to *Chapter 4*, specifically the section, *Presence in the Classroom*.

- Remember the 6 project categories: **Reflection, Express, Explore, Empower, Expand** and **Freedom** and how they relate to **The 3 Rules**. *(pg. 125)*

- The curriculum is designed to build on the experience of previous projects so if possible, do the Full Schedule.

- Choose a project schedule, Fundamentals or Claiming Face Full schedule, or choose individual projects according to what you feel your class needs. Use the planning tools to help you. *(pgs. 125-127)*

- Projects take about 40 mins to an hour but can be expanded or broken up if desired.

- Familiarize yourself with the symbols to make implementing the projects easier.

- Print enough copies of photos and handouts for the school year according to your desired project schedule. Here is a quick list of photos/handouts needed based on class size of 30 students:

Fundamentals Schedule:

    15 - Making Face handout #1 on cardstock
    15 - Making Face handout #2 on cardstock
    30 - Rule #1 handout on cardstock
    30 - Frida handout on cardstock
    30 - Rule #2 handout on cardstock
    30 - Rule #3 handout on cardstock
    "Regular" photo (1 of each student) = 30 student photos on cardstock
    "Wild" photo (1 of each student) = 30 student photos on cardstock

CLAIMING FACE **Full Schedule:**

  September - January (First photo shoot of students)
    15 - Making Face handout #1 on cardstock
    15 - Making Face handout #2 on cardstock
    30 - Frida handout on cardstock
    "Regular" photo (1 of each student) = 30 student photos on cardstock
    "Wild" photo (1 of each student) = 30 student photos on cardstock
    30 - Rule #1 handout on cardstock
    30 - Rule #2 handout on cardstock

  January - June (Second photo shoot of students)
    30 - Rule #3 handout on cardstock
    "Regular" photo (4 of each student) = 120 student photos on cardstock
    All of Me Option 1: 4 "Regular" photo on 1 page of cardstock for each student = 30
    All of Me Option 2: "Regular" photo (4 of each student) = 120 on cardstock

***Note that this is just the minimum, you may want extra copies on hand

The CLAIMING FACE
Glossary

ARTIST (n.)

Creativity is the teacher that lives within each of us. Being an artist means that no matter what activity we are engaged in, we are listening to and guided by our inner teacher. —found on pg. 13

TO CLAIM FACE (v.)

(1) to recognize and assert one's place/face and inherent belonging in the world; (2) to embrace and celebrate what one's face expresses, how it reflects one's life and historical context in relation to ethnicity, gender expression, individuality, selfhood and more; (3) to declare and require in community the birthright to be exactly who one is inside and out; (4) to know one's self inside and out. —found on pg. 9

COURAGE (n.)

means that you are afraid. You are aware of your fear. And you make enough room for your fear to exist within you while you do what you know is right for you in the moment. —found on pg. 52

CREATIVITY (n.)

Creativity is the personal teacher within each of us. As our birthright it is the inherent ability and energy, we as humans are born with, to transcend current ideas, forms and patterns and to create meaningful new ones that are relevant to the moment and our deepest selves. This allows us to connect with, maintain and perpetuate flow and integrity with who we are at core. —found on pg. 1

ENERGY (n.)

the creative force, the momentum within ALL things. Energy can transform, but it cannot be created or destroyed. It is constant. Quantum Physics is beginning to show us that EVERYTHING at the most fundamental level is made up of energy. —found on pg. 40

Glossary

TO EXPRESS (v.)

to allow your internal experience to be manifested externally in some way for you and others to witness.—found on pg.65

FREEDOM (n.)

(1) The power to exercise choice and make decisions without constraint from within or without. (2) To allow an unencumbered flow of energy to move through one's self and life.—found on pg.37

POLKA_DOT (n.)

Our most basic mark. In this simple mark we see our unique self in how we hold our stories in our hand, how we hold a pencil, contact the page, and create.—found on pg.75

PRESENCE (n.)

Buddhists call it mindfulness. Scientists call it being observant. Body psychotherapists call it witnessing or awareness. Presence, Awareness, Paying Attention, Witnessing, Observation, Mindfulness. These are all words that mean paying attention to our actions, thoughts, feelings, surroundings and interactions in each moment. Presence is our full awareness of our experience in the moment. —found on pg.49

REFLECTION (n.) TO REFLECT (v.)

(1) An image outside of us that replicates either our actual image, as in a mirror or shows us something about ourselves, as in art, or the sunset. (2) To pause and focus one's attention in careful consideration on a thought or image.—found on pg.25

RESPECT (n.)

Is awareness of and admiration for someone who is being true to their deepest, most creative self. It never remains a one sided experience but always transforms into a circular or reciprocal experience, because as we admire others being true to themselves, we ourselves change and become more true to our deepest, most creative self. This results in self-respect and continues the cycle for others to then see us and be transformed. And so on. Respect leads to self-respect. Self-respect leads to respect.—found on pg.56

Glossary

TO SELF-EMPOWER (v.)

Deriving the strength to do something through one's own thoughts and based on the belief that one knows what is best for oneself.—found on pg. 66

SELF-PORTRAIT (n.)

an image created of one's self with the purpose of expressing experience, claiming self, creating reflection and knowing one's self more deeply.—found on pg. 128

TO TRUST (v.)

to relax into ourselves, the moment, and our lives and know that we can listen to ourselves and always find our way.—found on pg. 38

UNIVERSAL REFLECTION (n.)

Reflection is usually defined as an image or representation. Reflection becomes Universal when it is not dependent on image, but on action between two or more people. For example, when the educator and the student both do the Claiming Face projects, they create a Universal Reflection of each other both being engaged in the creative process.—found on pg. 11

WITNESS (n.)

A person who sees and pays close attention to either one's self or another. Witnessing strengthens the vitality of existence and presence of the one who is seen and has an effect on who is seen in accordance with intent. For example, if the seer's intent is to respect who they are seeing, then respect will become a relational factor. —found on pg. 29

Glossary

Artists

Faith Ringgold:

African American artist known for her painted story quilts, combining painting, quilted fabric and storytelling. She says of her work: *"Because the mask is your face, the face is a mask, so I'm thinking of the face as a mask because of the way I see faces is coming from an African vision of the mask which is the thing that we carry around with us, it is our presentation, it's our front, it's our face."*

Frida Kahlo:

the handout for the *Frida Mirror* ***comes from the book Frida Kahlo: Brush of Anguish*** (Paperback) by Martha Zamora.

One of the most influential Mexican painters of the middle twentieth century. She had an amazing focus on self-portraiture.

Jackson Pollock:

American Painter who created a technique of pouring and dripping paint that is thought to be one of the origins of the term action painting. He says of his painting: *"When I am in my painting, I'm not aware of what I'm doing. It is only after a sort of 'get acquainted' period that I see what I have been about. I have no fear of making changes, destroying the image, etc., because the painting has a life of its own. I try to let it come through."*

Marc Chagall:

Russian-French Artist, one of the most successful artists of the 20th century. His *"vision soared and he created a new reality, one that drew on both his inner and outer worlds."* Because he was Jewish during a very difficult time for Jews, Chagall had to make a choice between hiding or claiming who he was. He chose to *"cherish and publically express (his) Jewish roots"* by integrating them into his art.

Mary Cassatt:

American artist who often created images of the social and private lives of women, with particular emphasis on the intimate bonds between mothers and children. She was determined to make a living as an artist, highly unusual for a woman of her era. She worked extensively in pastels.

Picasso:

Spanish painter, draftsman, and sculptor. He is one of the most recognized figures in 20th-century art. Radically and wildly inventive, he took the idea of portraiture apart and changed the way we see.

Romare Bearden:

African American Artist- Recognized as one of the most creative and original visual artists of the twentieth century. He experimented with many different mediums and artistic styles, but is best known for his richly textured collages. Bearden grew as an artist not by learning how to create new techniques and mediums, but by his life experiences. The different decades he created art and the different events that took place completely reshaped his vision of art.

Art Materials

Blick Art Materials
http://www.dickblick.com; 1-800-828-4548

With its large online selection and local stores in 15 states and more opening soon, Blick offers great discounts on art supplies. Become a preferred customer and save 10% on your purchases, free to sign-up for students and teachers. Blick also offers school discounts, visit their customer service link to find out more information. To help introduce art into the early years of school, they developed a new catalog directed to K-6 grade levels. This site is filled with lots of resources for educators including lesson plans, an educator forum, and more. Check out their Teacher News section: **http://www.dickblick.com/landing/teachernews.**

Cheap Joe's Art Stuff: "Make more art. Spend less money."
http://www.cheapjoes.com; 1-800-277-2788

Beyond art supplies at wonderfully cheap prices, you'll also find tons of useful information, tips, and discussions about how to use different materials, including art workshops. Check out the "community" tab for discussion forum, links and other great resources. If you are in the North Carolina area you can visit their outlet store or sign up for their e-mail newsletter to receive exclusive savings online.

Homeroom Teacher: Arts & Crafts Supplies
http://www.homeroomteacher.com/artsandcrafts.aspx; **1-800-828-4548**

Wide selection of art supplies, kits, art storage and more with up to 60% off retail prices.

Office Depot: Star Teacher Rewards Program
http://www.mystarteacher.com

Free to join and you get back a certain percentage of what you buy which allows you to get more art supplies for free. With this program you also get an instant **discount of 15% on copies and printing** which could be useful when needing student photos. Office Depot also has a program to earn free school supplies with their *5% Back to Schools Program*

Prang Power: Earn FREE Art Supplies for your School
http://www.prangpower.com

Enroll your school in this program and when you save and submit UPC codes from Prang, Dixon, or Ticonderoga products you earn points toward free art supplies.

Staples: Staples Rewards Teacher
http://www.staplesrewardscenter.com

Free to join and 10% back on art supplies and copy and print purchases, plus free delivery on orders over $50.

Art Skills

***Art Is Fundamental: Teaching the Elements and Principles
of Art in Elementary School* (Paperback)**
by Eileen S. Prince, Published by Zephyr Press
Art curriculum for elementary students but can be easily adapted for middle
or high school students. Includes lesson plans divided by a particular topic:
color, value, texture, shape, line and form.

Art for Creative Kids
http://abrakadoodle.blogspot.com
This blog is dedicated to ideas, trends and activities that develop creative art
skills in children.

***Discovering Great Artists: Hands-On Art for Children in the Styles
of the Great Masters* (Bright Ideas for Learning) (Paperback)**
by Maryanne F. Kohl and Kim Solga, Published by Bright Ring Publishing
This book contains more than 150 activities to teach the styles, works, and
techniques of the great masters—Van Gogh, Michelangelo, Rembrandt, and
more.

***Drawing Faces: Internet-linked* (Usborne Art Ideas) (Paperback)**
by Rosie Dickens, Jan McCafferty , Fiona Watt, Carrie A. Seay, illustrated by
Howard Allman, Published by E.D.C. Publishing
This book explores drawing faces in all different mediums, pencil, watercolor,
collage, and more.

***Dynamic Art Projects for Children: Includes Step-by-step Instructions
And Photographs* (Spiral-bound)**
by Denise M. Logan, Published by Crystal Productions
This book contains the art curriculum at the Gilbert, AZ, Elementary School
System that teaches students how to use their own creativity.

***How the Art Center Enhances Children's Development* Article**
http://www.education.com/reference/article/art-center-enhances-children-
development/
Article that explores the benefits and development of life skills that engaging
in art promotes. *"Art enhances creativity, which is crucial for innovation
and adaptation. Creative people have the ability to see multiple solutions to
a problem, employ original thoughts, and use their imagination. As a field,
art promotes these skills, encouraging unique and divergent responses and
diverse ways of looking at things."*

Monart Drawing Schools
http://www.monart.com; 510-350-7402
Monart is more than a method that teaches people how to draw. Leading
educators recognize Monart as a way students can use several learning
modalities by teaching them how to focus and concentrate, make decisions,
solve problems, plan sequence, and develop hand-eye coordination.

Resources by Topic

Creativity

Art & Learning to Think & Feel
http://www.goshen.edu/art/ed/art-ed-links.html
A website by Marvin Bartel, Ed. D.
Emeritus Professor of Art at Goshen College in Indiana
Wealth of information on this website, his essay on *"Ten Classroom Creativity Killers"* provides some interesting insights on creativity in the classroom.

Creativity in the curriculum
http://www.teachingexpertise.com/articles/creativity-in-the-curriculum-1561
A school with creativity at the heart of the learning process will benefit by increasing the motivation of staff and pupils, says former head, Dave Weston. In this article and case study, he shows the way to more imaginative approaches to curriculum planning.

Cross Training: Arts and Academics Are Inseparable
http://www.edutopia.org/cross-training
"At the Boston Arts Academy...there's nothing dispensable about singing -- or dancing, acting, drawing, and painting. The arts at this public school are central to the mission of educating students in math, science, and the humanities."

E. Paul Torrance (known as The Father of Creativity):
http://www.coe.uga.edu/coenews/2003/EPTorranceObit.html
Torrance was a UGA Professor Emeritus of Educational Psychology who invented the benchmark method for quantifying creativity and created the platform for all research on the subject since. The *"Torrance Tests of Creative Thinking"* helped shatter the theory that IQ tests alone were sufficient to gauge real intelligence. The tests solidified what previously was only conceptual – namely that creative levels can be scaled and then increased through practice.

***What is Creativity?* Article**
http://curriculum.qcda.gov.uk/key-stages-1-and-2/learning-across-the-curriculum/creativity/whatiscreativity/index.aspx
Article that begins to look at creativity, why it's important, how teachers can promote it and more. *"A good starting point for defining creativity is 'All our futures: Creativity, culture and education', the National Advisory Committee's report (DfEE, 1999). This report states that we are all, or can be, creative to a lesser or greater degree if we are given the opportunity."*

Resources by Topic

Education & Educators

A. S. Neill: *Summerhill: A Radical Approach to Child-Rearing*

Neill believed that the happiness of the child should be the paramount consideration in decisions about the child's upbringing, and that this happiness grew from a sense of personal freedom. He felt that deprivation of this sense of freedom during childhood, and the consequent unhappiness experienced by the repressed child, was responsible for many of the psychological disorders of adulthood.

EdChange
http://www.edchange.org

Mission: *EdChange is dedicated to diversity and equity in ourselves, our schools, and our society. We act to shape schools and communities in which all people, regardless of race, gender, sexual orientation, class, (dis)ability, language, or religion, have equitable opportunities to achieve to their fullest and to be safe, valued, affirmed, and empowered.*

Teaching Tolerance
http://www.tolerance.org

One of the primary goals of Teaching Tolerance is to advance and support the creation of inclusive and equitable K-12 school communities. Disparities in academic achievement and educational access demonstrate the need for improved preparation and support for classroom teachers.

Understanding Prejudice
http://www.understandingprejudice.org/teach

UnderstandingPrejudice.org was established in 2002 with funding from the National Science Foundation (Grant Number 9950517) and McGraw-Hill Higher Education. The purpose of the site is to offer educational resources and information on prejudice, discrimination, multiculturalism, and diversity, with the ultimate goal of reducing the level of intolerance and bias in contemporary society. Their Teacher's Corner has classroom activities, teaching tips and more.

Sonia Nieto
http://en.wikipedia.org/wiki/Sonia_Nieto

One of the leading authors and teachers in the field of multiculturalism.

coAction Connection: *be safe. be diverse. belong*
http://www.coactionconnection.com

Mission: *coAction Connection provides impactful learning experiences and tools to individuals and organizations enabling people to build common ground and new understandings across cultural differences. Our work builds the capacity within individuals to engage effectively in dialogues of multiple perspectives. This leads to the creation of communities and organizations imbedded with cultural Intelligence.*

Resources by Topic

Presence

Peter Levine: Somatic Experiencing Books:
Waking the Tiger: Healing Trauma
Trauma-Proofing Your Kids: A Parents' Guide for Instilling Confidence, Joy and Resilience

Somatic Experiencing® is a body-awareness approach to trauma being taught throughout the world. It is the result of over forty years of observation, research, and hands-on development by Dr. Levine. Based upon the realization that human beings have an innate ability to overcome the effects of trauma, Somatic Experiencing has touched the lives of many thousands. SE® restores self-regulation, and returns a sense of aliveness, relaxation and wholeness to traumatized individuals who have had these precious gifts taken away.

Janet Adler: Authentic Movement Books:
Offering from the Conscious Body
The Discipline of Authentic Movement

Janet Adler, with a Ph.D. in Mystical Studies, teaches the discipline of Authentic Movement in the United States and Europe and was the founder and director of The Mary Starks Whitehouse Institute, the first school devoted to the study and practice of the discipline. She is the author of *Arching Backward* and of two films: *Looking for Me*, documenting her work with autistic children, and *Still Looking*, reflecting her work in the discipline of Authentic Movement.

Eckhart Tolle: Presence Books: *The Power of Now, A New Earth*

Eckhart's profound yet simple teachings have already helped countless people throughout the world find inner peace and greater fulfillment in their lives. At the core of the teachings lies the transformation of consciousness, a spiritual awakening that he sees as the next step in human evolution. An essential aspect of this awakening consists in transcending our ego-based state of consciousness. This is a prerequisite not only for personal happiness but also for the ending of violent conflict endemic on our planet.

Mindfulness (another word for Presence)

http://www.shambhala.com/html/learn/features/buddhism/basics/mindfulness.cfm

Mindfulness is mirror-thought. It reflects only what is presently happening and in exactly the way it is happening. There are no biases.

Jane Roberts: Author, poet and psychic: some quotes:

"When you affirm your own rightness in the universe, then you co-operate with others easily and automatically as part of your own nature. You, being yourself, helps others be themselves. Because you recognize your own uniqueness you will not need to dominate others, nor cringe before them"
"You are here to aid in the Great Expansion of consciousness. You are not here to cry about the miseries of the human condition, but to change them when you find them not to your liking through the joy, strength and vitality that is within you; to create the spirit as faithfully and beautifully as you can in flesh."

Statistics

CLASS REFLECTION

When I researched some of the stressors that affect our children, I was moved when I saw the numbers, especially when I contextualized them as a classroom. Note the racial backdrop of the class. Your classes may vary. Percentage-wise I have worked with relatively few white children.

In seeing these numbers, first and foremost I was struck by the strength and resilience I have witnessed over the years. I have been unaware of specific statistics until I did this research, but I could always sense that much of the art the children created was helping them navigate experiences like these. Through the CLAIMING FACE curriculum, I believe it is important for us to know and be present with all that we are. As I shared at the beginning: *"if I claimed my own face, I was taking a step toward claiming all of myself in every deep and superficial way. In this way my face could not be held against me, by me nor anyone else."*

Class of 30 students (half girls/half boys)
(Statistics are based on current population average)

66% White=19-20 students

15% Latino=4-5 students

14% African American=4 students

5% Asian=1-2 students

Statistically the number of children in a class dealing with the following:
(If your class has a higher Latino and/or African American representation then statistics show that the stressors with an asterisk (*) will most likely be higher.)

1 :homeless*

1 :parent in prison*

2-3 :parent under correctional supervision*

7-8 :hunger*

6-12 :living in poverty*

1 :foster care

1 :physically abused

1-2 :witness domestic violence

2 :boy child sexual abuse

3-4 :girl child sexual abuse

3-4 :exposed to alcohol or drug abuse

3-4 :parent with mental/emotional instability

Resources by Topic

Statistics

There are a number of other possible stressors, such as learning disabilities, serious injury or health issues, the complexities of immigration, English as a second language, bullies, family dysfunction, physical disability, the 3 kinds of racism: personally-mediated, internalized, and institutional, homophobia, transphobia, sexism and so on.

<u>Books that could be used to contextualize some stresses:</u>
(Refer to *Chapter 8, Books: Behind the Story*)

> *On My Block* :physical stress (such as an accident)
>
> *Nana's Big Surprise* :grief
>
> *My Colors, My World* :depression, dissociation related to difficult experience

SOURCE STATISTICS
***Descriptions taken directly from listed website*

Overall

America's Children: Key National Indicators of Well-Being, 2009
<u>http://www.childstats.gov/americaschildren</u>
The report presents 40 key indicators on important aspects of children's lives drawn from our most reliable statistics, objectively based on substantial research, and representative of large segments of the population rather than one particular group.

Abuse

Child Sexual Abuse Statistics
<u>http://www.darknesstolight.org/KnowAbout/statistics_2.asp</u>
- 1 in 4 girls is sexually abused before the age of 18
- 1 in 6 boys is sexually abused before the age of 18

Child Abuse Statistics
<u>http://www.findcounseling.com/journal/child-abuse/child-abuse-statistics.html</u>
The problem is large and is increasing. Saying anything beyond that seems meaningless. Every attempt to measure incidence to date has been flawed. The estimates range from less than 5 percent to more than 40 percent of all children. The National Center on Child Abuse and Neglect (NCCAN), part of the U.S. Dept. of Health and Human Services compiles data about the number of cases reported to Child Protective Services (CPS) each year, but the fact is the number of reported cases is small compared with the number of actual cases. We can reason this by looking at several studies which asked adults about childhood abuse. Adults are more likely to report their own childhood abuse because they no longer live in fear of immediate retaliation from the abuser and they have had time to recover from the psychological effects of living in an abusive household.

Statistics

Addiction

Children of Addicted Parents: Important Facts

http://www.hopenetworks.org/addiction/Children%20of%20Addicts.htm

Alcoholism and other drug addiction have genetic and environmental causes. Both have serious consequences for children who live in homes where parents are involved. More than 28 million Americans are children of alcoholics; nearly 11 million are under the age of 18. This figure is magnified by the countless number of others who are affected by parents who are impaired by other psychoactive drugs.

Alcoholism Statistics

http://www.alcoholism-information.com/Alcoholism_Statistics.html

• Approximately one in four children is exposed to family alcoholism, addiction, or alcohol abuse some time before the age of 18.

Domestic Violence

Domestic Violence Statistics

http://www.turningpointservices.org

Between 3 and 10 million American children witness domestic violence each year.

Foster Care

Foster Care Statistics

http://www.childwelfare.gov/pubs/factsheets/foster.cfm#key

On September 30, 2006, there were an estimated 510,000 children in foster care.

Homelessness

Homeless Children and Youth

http://www.nationalhomeless.org/factsheets/education.html

Families with children are by most accounts among the fastest growing segments of the homeless population. In the United States an estimated 1.35 million from 600 thousand families will experience homelessness today, while 3.8 million more will live in "precarious housing situations." [1] Put another way, of every 200 children in America, 3 will be homeless today and more than double that number will be at risk for homelessness. [2]

Hunger

Hunger Statistics

http://www.washingtonpost.com/wp-dyn/content/article/2009/11/16/AR2009111601598.html

About 12.4 million children (17 percent of all children) lived in households that were classified as food insecure at times in 2007. About 691,000 of these children (0.9 percent of all children) lived in households classified as having very low food security among children.

Resources by Topic

Statistics

Mental Disorders

Mental Disorders in America

http://www.nimh.nih.gov/health/publications/the-numbers-count-mental-disorders-in-america/index.shtml

Mental disorders are common in the United States and internationally. An estimated 26.2 percent of Americans ages 18 and older — about one in four adults — suffer from a diagnosable mental disorder in a given year.1 When applied to the 2004 U.S. Census residential population estimate for ages 18 and older, this figure translates to 57.7 million people.

Parent in Prison

Parents in Prison

http://bjs.ojp.usdoj.gov/content/pub/press/pptmcpr.cfm

About 2.3 percent of the 74 million children in the U.S. resident population who were under the age of 18 on July 1, 2007, had a parent in prison. Black and Hispanic children were about eight and three times, respectively, more likely than white children to have a parent in prison. Among minor children in the U.S. resident population, 6.7 percent of black children, 2.4 percent of Hispanic children, and 0.9 percent of white children had a parent in prison. State inmates who were parents reported that nearly a quarter of their children were age four or younger and reported having two children on average.

http://www.connectforkids.org/node/4358

More than 7 million children have a parent under some form of correctional supervision, Bureau of Justice Statistics

Poverty

Poverty & food wastage in America Statistics

http://www.soundvision.com/Info/poor/statistics.asp

35.9 million people live below the poverty line in America, including 12.9 million children.

Racism

Racism related to Economics

http://www2.newsadvance.com/lna/news/local/article/todays_racism_related_to_economics_duke_professor_says/22004

Explicit, overt racism is now out of fashion. Indeed, all signs are that we are moving closer to becoming a colorblind society in many ways. But, said Bonilla-Silva, racism is really more about economics than *"whether we can sit down and have a beer with each other."*

The economic inequities between black and white have changed little over the past few decades, Bonilla-Silva continued. And it is the acceptance of these inequities that provides the core of the new racism. Instead of *"you're*

Statistics

not as good as we are," it has become *"you're as good as we are, but you're not going to get any of what we have."*

The State of Minorities: The Recession Issue

http://www.americanprogress.org/issues/2009/01/state_of_minorities.html

The United States entered its most severe recession in decades in 2008. Even before the recession hit, minorities were in a more precarious economic situation than whites, largely because of fewer good employment opportunities. As the economy and the labor market declined, so did the fortunes of American families, hitting minorities especially hard.

(**<u>*Please Note:*</u> *I found numerous references for the statistics listed here but only chose to list key ones, there are additional websites, books, etc that provide even more detailed statistics than what can be covered in this book.*)

Witnessing & Quantum Physics

Bruce Lipton

http://www.brucelipton.com/ :*Uncovering the Biology of Belief*

Bruce H Lipton, PhD is an internationally recognized authority in bridging science and spirit. He has been a guest speaker on dozens of TV and radio shows, as well as keynote presenter for national conferences. His most recent book, ***Spontaneous Evolution***, is available now.

Consciousness Project

http://consciousnessproject.org/articles/quantum-perspective-physiologic-response/

"When you witness something, it changes. At the quantum level, the choices you make—your intention—shifts the probability of a potentiality."

Quantum Physics and Manifestation

http://www.abundance-and-happiness.com/quantum-physics.html

This a wonderful article that discusses and explains, in easy to understand terms, the interconnectedness of life, how our thoughts and beliefs affect our reality and how that relates to discoveries in Quantum Physics.

Thinking Through the Body

http://www.thinkbody.co.uk/papers/embodying.htm

Article that discusses Authentic Movement as it relates to witnessing and its transformative effects. The words of body psychotherapist John Waterstone, writing about witnessing in supervision, are relevant here: *"In existential terms the fact of being seen is essential to the process of existence. The individual ex-ists, ie. stands out via the dynamic process of showing the self to the self and to others. The self is defined (comes into being) [...] by being /doing in the eyes of another, in the eyes of the self, and in the witnessing of the impact of the self on the other."*

Resources by Topic

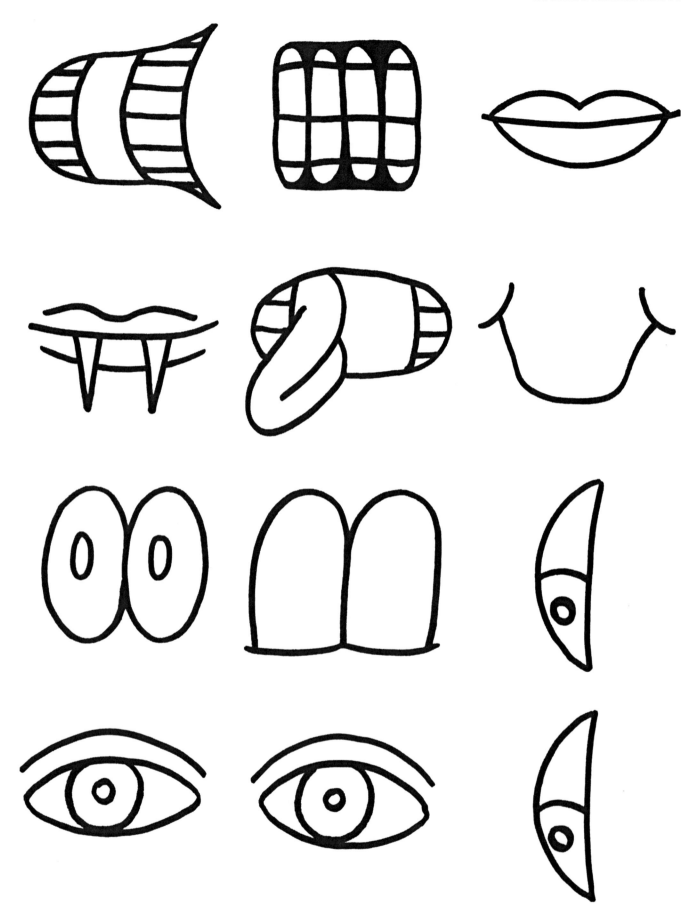

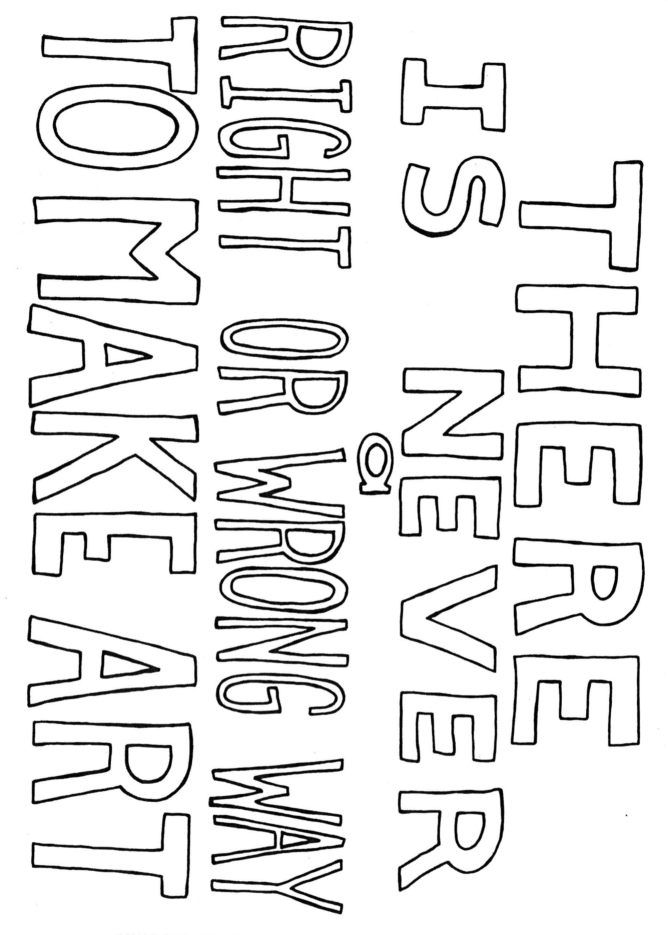

MAYA'S ESSAYS

Matching books and readers: Helping English learners in grades K-6
Essay by Maya *"I Know the River Loves Me"*
Edited by Nancy Hadaway and Terrell Young
Publisher: Guilford Press June 2010

Celebrating Cuentos: Promoting Latino Children's Literature and Literacy in Classrooms & Libraries
Essay by Maya *"I Am All That I See"*
Edited by Jaime Campbell Naidoo
Publisher: Libraries Unlimited, November 2010

SELECTED FINE ART BOOKS

Chicana Art: The Politics of Spiritual and Aesthetic Altarities
Author: Laura E.Pérez
Publisher: Duke University Press, June 2007

Triumph of Our Communities: Four Decades of Mexican American Art
Authors: Gary D. Keller, Amy Phillips
Publisher: Bilingual Review Press (AZ), April 2005

Chicano Art for Our Millennium
Authors: Mary Erickson, Pat Villeneuve, Gary D. Keller
Publisher: Bilingual Review Press (AZ), April 2004

Contemporary Chicana/o Art: Artists, Works, Culture and Education
Edited by Gary D. Keller
Publisher: Bilingual Review Press (AZ), September 2002

Fine Art Website: **www.mayagonzalez.com**

About the Author

Maya Christina Gonzalez is an award-winning artist, author, and educator. She has made a tremendous amount of art for nearly 20 children's books and, with each and every book, is always thinking about the child who will one day hold that book in their hands. Author and illustrator of *My Colors, My World*, the 2008 Pura Belpré Honor Award winner, she has been going into schools and universities since 1996 teaching children and educators the importance of creativity as a tool for personal empowerment and the power of both internal and external reflection.

These lessons have culminated in her transformative work, CLAIMING FACE. The Educator's Guide, is the first book from this curriculum. A lifetime in the making, her curriculum gives insight and guides educators in implementing the tools of presence, creativity, and reflection in their lives and classrooms.

While her CLAIMING FACE curriculum began for her as a child and she sees it greatly benefiting children and the educators who work with them, she also sees the lessons of **self-empowerment through self-portraiture** reaching out to even more audiences. She is currently coordinating workshops in San Francisco for women to claim and know self, with aspirations to create another book specifically geared toward women. It is her hope that she can circulate this work to larger and larger circles reaching anyone with the irresistible desire to claim self and life.

Spoiled by getting to write her last two children's books, Maya is beginning to explore the power and promise of fairy tales, particularly for children dealing with multiple stresses. Maya sees the power of magical realism and imagination as a tool to understand and surmount challenging life lessons. Returning to Maya's love of writing and story telling, fairy tales seem a natural extension of the CLAIMING FACE sentiment. She is currently working on two tales for young adults, *Moon and the Mother Who Had No Bones,* and *The Girl Who Could See Colors.* Using potent metaphors and magical worlds, these tales beautifully illustrate the power of finding one's own inner strength and resources amidst challenging family dynamics and dysfunction.

She shows her personal paintings in San Francisco and the US and her fine art is featured in many art books, including the cover of *Contemporary Chicano/a Art*. Maya lives, plays, and makes lots of art in San Francisco with her husband Matthew, cofounder of Reflection Press, and her daughter Zai.

She hopes that one day all children, and all people, will be free to grow and evolve in a world where they are supported in claiming their most full authentic self and are respected and loved for exactly who they are.

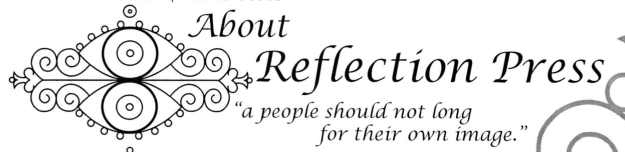

About *Reflection Press*

*"a people should not long
for their own image."*

Our Mission

Reflection Press empowers people to fully claim themselves and their inherent creative force. By providing experiences and materials that use creativity, presence, and reflection as tools to find, explore, and know self, we strengthen ourselves as a people. In this strength, we come to know that we all belong here and now and that we all possess the capacity to create a world based on equality in which we are free to express and expand into our truest selves.

Who We Are

Reflection Press was founded to support people in using creativity to more deeply know and celebrate themselves. Rooted in the life work of cofounder Maya Christina Gonzalez, artist, author, and educator, Reflection Press is committed to providing experiences and materials to empower people to create their own authentic reflections when external ones do not accurately exist. Reflection, seeing ourselves in the world around us, is a first and important step in knowing that we belong, we are here and we are not alone. In addition, using the lessons of presence and awareness, people learn to sustain the flow of creative energy and better understand their experience and self. Together these practices aim to strengthen a sense of self which helps us to learn, make supportive choices, respect ourselves and those around us, and care about our lives and ultimately our world.

What We Offer

Reflection Press provides workshops, presentations, lectures and curriculum that engage the creative force as a tool for self-empowerment. We also work to provide imagery, written and visual, that begins to reflect people who are often under-represented in the current media. Through books, posters, prints, and online resources, we strive to reach and empower as many people as possible.

Thank you for playing with us!

Visit us online at www.reflectionpress.com

Be sure to check our website regularly for additional resources, updates, and extras to expand and deepen your study of our CLAIMING FACE curriculum!

Give the Gift of CLAIMING FACE to your Friends and Colleagues

Order online at www.claimingface.com or use this form.

☐ YES, I want _____ copies of **CLAIMING FACE: Self-Empowerment through Self-Portraiture** for $39.95 each.

☐ YES, I am interested in having Maya speak or give a seminar to my school or organization. Please send me information.

☐ YES, subscribe me to the Reflection Press email list for updates regarding our curriculum, what we have to offer and updates about the press. My email address is: _____.

Include $6.00 shipping and handling for one book, and $1.00 for each additional book.

California residents must add 8.25% sales tax.

Orders must be in US dollars. Payment must accompany order. Allow 3 weeks for delivery.

☐ My check or money order for $ _____ is enclosed.

☐ Please charge my: ☐ Visa   ☐ Mastercard   ☐ American Express

Name _____

School/Organization _____

City/State/Zip _____

Phone_____Email _____

Card Number _____

Expiration Date_____Signature _____

Make your check payable and return to:

Reflection Press
3543 18th St. #17
San Francisco, CA 94110

www.reflectionpress.com
www.claimingface.com
Email: info@reflectionpress.com
Phone: (415) 503-0076

"Everything begins with yourself."

"I am here. I belong."

Breinigsville, PA USA
09 April 2010
235836BV00002B/1/P